CW00558284

# The Leadership of
# MUHAMMAD

# The Leadership of
# MUHAMMAD

## JOHN ADAIR

LONDON  PHILADELPHIA  NEW DELHI

**Publisher's note**

Every possible effort has been made to ensure that the information contained in this book is accurate at the time of going to press, and the publishers and author cannot accept responsibility for any errors or omissions, however caused. No responsibility for loss or damage occasioned to any person acting, or refraining from action, as a result of the material in this publication can be accepted by the editor, the publisher or the author.

First published in Great Britain and the United States in 2010 by Kogan Page Limited

| | | |
|---|---|---|
| 120 Pentonville Road | 525 South 4th Street, #241 | 4737/23 Ansari Road |
| London N1 9JN | Philadelphia PA 19147 | Daryaganj |
| United Kingdom | USA | New Delhi 110002 |
| www.koganpage.com | | India |

© John Adair, 2010

The right of John Adair to be identified as the author of this work has been asserted by him in accordance with the Copyright, Designs and Patents Act 1988.

ISBN      978 0 7494 6076 1
E-ISBN   978 0 7494 6116 4

**British Library Cataloguing-in-Publication Data**

A CIP record for this book is available from the British Library.

**Library of Congress Cataloging-in-Publication Data**

Adair, John Eric, 1934-
  The leadership of Muhammad / John Adair.
     p. cm.
  Includes index.
    ISBN 978-0-7494-6076-1 -- ISBN 978-0-7494-6116-4 (ebook)  1. Leadership. 2. Muhammad, Prophet, d. 632 3. Bedouins--Jordan--Social life and customs. I. Title.
  HD57.7.A34 2010
  658.4'092--dc22
                              2010002760

Typeset by Saxon Graphics Ltd, Derby
Printed and bound in Great Britain
Manufacturing managed by Jellyfish Print Solutions Ltd

On a journey
the lord of a people is their servant.

**Muhammad**

# CONTENTS

# INTRODUCTION

*As you are so will be the rulers that rule you.*

ARAB PROVERB

This book is a biographical inquiry into one aspect of the Prophet Muhammad's life: his leadership. It is not a full biography of Muhammad. If you are not familiar with his story you will find a brief outline of it at the end of this book. Consequently I do no more than touch lightly upon aspects of Muhammad's life that any biographer would regard as central, such as his roles as Messenger and Prophet.

Having just used the word *role* I should say 'up front' that I regard it as the key concept for understanding leadership. A role is by origin a part taken by an actor in a play, but in our wider use it means a person's characteristic or expected function. There is a case for saying that it is the expectations of people that determine a particular role in a human group or society. Notice also a phrase introduced relatively recently into the English language, *role model*: a person who is regarded by others as an outstandingly good example of a particular role.

For Muslims, the first and original leader is God, and all are bound by their faith to obey God's law. Thus any leader of any organization – business, political or religious – is also first and foremost a follower of God. This fact imposes limits on Islamic leaders, and defines their duties to the people they lead. In Islamic thought, model leaders were simultaneously both exalted and humble, capable of vision and inspiration, yet at the same time dedicated to the service of their people.

As you read these pages you will, I hope, be able to judge for yourself just how close Muhammad comes to this ideal. My argument in this book is that this ideal – glimpsed more than once in the life of the Prophet Muhammad – accords well with what we now know to be the universal truth about the nature and practice of leadership.

I believe that there is a universal or generic role of *leader*. Moreover, thanks to one lucky discovery (see Chapter 8), I have come as close as anyone has yet been to defining what that universal or generic role actually is. When experimentally applied on a large scale to selection and training of leaders the theory has worked consistently, and it has done so for over half a century. That is why I now claim that it is *true*.

Just as this book is not a biography of Muhammad, neither is it a manual on leadership. My method of writing is to complete each chapter with a set of key points. A pearl is formed around a grain of sand. Think of each key point as a grain of sand that – if you coat it in time with quiet reflections from your own experience and values – will become for you a pearl, lustrous and iridescent. Then it will be *your* pearl of wisdom.

If I may add a personal note: at the age of 20 I was fortunate to serve for a year as adjutant of a Bedouin regiment in the Arab Legion, as the army of the Hashemite Kingdom of Jordan was then known. Arab Legion was an apt name then, however, because the 900 Bedouin officers and soldiers of the Ninth Regiment came from all the tribes of greater Arabia. The Arabic name I was given on joining the regiment in Jerusalem in 1954, and by which I was known, has remained with me ever since – Sweillim. It is not a given name, but an affectionate form of Salman or Suleiman mainly found among the Bedouin tribes in the north of Saudi Arabia. You will, I hope, find my affection for my Bedouin companions of long ago reflected in these pages.

*The Messenger of God is an excellent model for those of you who put your hope in God and the Last Day and remember Him often.*

Q33:21

# In the Black Tents of
# BANI SA'D

*Truly, I am the most perfect Arab among you. My descent is from the Quraysh, and my tongue of the Bani Sa'd.*

MUHAMMAD

Early one morning in 570 CE a Bedouin man and his wife left the town of Mecca heading north-east to their camping grounds in the Najd, a great desert area in central Arabia to the north of the Nefud and the Rub'al Khali regions that forms a plateau of about 1,500 metres (5,000 feet) high. Al-Harith ibn Abd al-Uzza of the Bani Sa'd, a section of the much larger Bani Hawazin tribe, rode on his camel, and his wife Halima bint Abdallah followed on a donkey carrying her baby son Abdallah and an eight-day-old baby of the Quraysh tribe from Mecca that she was bringing home to suckle – Muhammad.

After a journey of nine days they reached the black tents of the Bani Sa'd in a wadi, a dry river valley dotted with solitary acacia trees and some sparse pasture for the flocks of sheep and goats. Once they were near the tent Halima's young daughters Unaysa and Judama (or Shayna, as she is called in other sources) – 'the girl with the beauty spot' – rushed out with cries of excitement to greet the return of their parents and brother and to make the acquaintance of their new baby foster-brother. Judama, the older of the two, would later remember helping her mother in the days that followed by carrying the baby Muhammad around on her hip.

The long and low desert nomads' tent that was to be Muhammad's home was made from strips of coarse cloth woven by the women from goats' hair, which gave it the distinctive black or dark-brown hue familiar to travellers down the ages. Called in Arabic a *bayt ash-sha'ar*, 'house of hair', it was divided into two by a low curtain separating the sleeping quarters – also the domain of the women and children – from the master's quarters (Arabic: *manzil*), where the master of the tent entertained other men – his relatives or guests – or if alone shared meals with his wife and children. This half of the tent would be furnished with camel-saddles, camel saddle-bags and cushions around the central hearth where the blackened cooking vessels and gleaming brass coffee pots stood ready for service.

Muhammad's earliest memories as a child included playing with the lambs that chased each other about or lay inert in the shade under the eaves of the tent. These lambs were too young to follow their mothers in the main flock. Led by the shepherds, the flock wandered for hours in the heat of the day over several miles, nibbling the odd blades of grass or vegetation. Muhammad had a particular fondness for the more agile goats, as well as for the half-wild cats that chased the desert scorpions and other unwelcome visitors around the tent's guy ropes. In later life Muhammad, according to legend, once cut a square out of his cloak to avoid disturbing a sleeping cat, such was his affection for them.

Muhammad appears to have stayed with Halima's family until he was 5 or 6 years old, although sometimes foster-children remained with their Bedouin foster-parents until they were 9 or 10 years. The chief reason given for this old custom among Meccans of farming out their baby sons to Bedouin foster-mothers was health: children brought up in the open-sided black tents were generally hardy and robust, whereas those reared in the crowded and unsanitary houses were exposed to lethal fevers and pestilence. The dry, clean air of the desert on the Najd plateau, the constant fresh wind and the healing sun kept the tents of the desert nomads such as the Bani Hawazin relatively free of disease. Both Muhammad's natural father and his natural mother would die young of fever in Mecca, leaving him an orphan before he was 7 or 8. No wonder that his Bedouin mother Halima meant so much to him.

But below the surface there is a deeper motive why the Quraysh noble families sent their babies to be fostered in Bedouin tents. All Arabs know that by origin they are desert nomads, tent-dwellers and herders of camels, sheep and goats, migrants in the vast land of Arabia. Their values, culture and language are all the products – as it were – from that aboriginal life of freedom in the black and brown goatskin tents of their forebears. Those who would be leaders of the Arabs, tradition suggested, should have Bedouin milk in them as well as the Bedouin blood in their veins that they shared with all Arabs.

The Bedouin – still the vast majority of Arabs in Muhammad's day – were also regarded, at least by themselves, as the purest and noblest of the Arab people. When a Meccan town-dweller made a slighting remark about the desert nomad tribes to a visiting Bedouin chief, the chief dismissed the remark with dignified contempt, for the Bedouin of the great ancient tribes knew themselves to be second to none on earth, equal if not superior to those tribes like the Quraysh who had left the desert for the mud-brick or stone-built houses of the few small towns and oases.

Both Abu Bakr and Umar, the first and second caliphs, as the successors of Muhammad were known, had the same experience of being reared by Bedouin foster-parents in their desert tents. Once, for example, when Umar rode through a wadi called Dajnan in the desert east of Mecca, its familiar landscape stirred in him a memory of those distant days of a childhood among the Bedouin.

'There was a time,' he recalled to his companions, 'when I roamed the desert as a camel-herd, dressed in a fleece jacket, and whenever I sat down tired my father would beat me. Now I live in a time when I need reckon none my superior except God!'

The example of Muhammad – the perfect Arab in the eyes of Muslims – helped to perpetuate the tradition of noble families giving their male babies into the care of Bedouin foster-parents. In the 19th century, for example, the practice was still common among the *Sharifs* (Arabic: honoured, high-born), those families in Mecca who claimed to be in the line of direct descent from Muhammad, such as the Hashemites. Other prominent Arabic ruling families also followed the custom. The present Emir of Qatar, for example, like the Prophet had a Bedouin foster-mother. What the future *amir* (Arabic: commander, leader) absorbed with his Bedouin mother's milk was a knowledge of the ways and manners of the Bedouin – the people the ruling families would govern in peace and command in battle. In Arabic these manners – the customary, well-trodden path of tradition, or normative rule – are called *sunna*.

After his return to Mecca and the death within two or three years of his natural mother Amina, Muhammad was brought up first in the house of his grandfather Abd al-Muttahib. When this man, whom Muhammad admired and revered, died he was passed on to another guardian, an uncle called Abu Talib.

Occasionally, the tradition tells us, Muhammad's Bedouin foster-mother Halima when visiting Mecca would call to see him. When Muhammad saw her coming towards their house, he would run out to meet her and welcome her warmly with 'Mother! Mother!' Leading her by hand into the house he would spread out his *abaya* – a wide, sleeveless cloak – on the floor and beckon her to sit on it with him, a Bedouin gesture of special reverence or respect reserved for an honoured guest. On one occasion later in life, during a drought year, Muhammad even persuaded his wealthy wife to give Halima a gift from them – a camel and 40 sheep.

One day – over 50 years later – Muhammad's second family among the Bani Sa'd were able to profit again from their claim on Muhammad's affections, for milk-brotherhood among the Bedouin is held to be as strong as blood-ties, the sacred bond of the tribe.

It came about like this. In February 630, more than 50 years after Muhammad's childhood doings in their tents, about 4,000 tribesmen from the Bani Hawazin ambushed a Muslim army almost three times their number. The Muslims had invited trouble by incautiously advancing along the narrow bottom of Wadi Hunayn without having sent out scouts. It was a natural place for an ambush. Suddenly, pouring down the hillsides from both sides, came down upon them the Hawazin warriors shouting their war cries. The charge of the Bedouin on camel and horseback, waving their lances and swords, caused panic in the Muslim ranks: the advance guard broke ranks and fled down the valley, straight into the main body, throwing them into confusion. The worst thing that infantry can do is to present their backs to the lances of the enemy horsemen as the Muslims were now doing. In a verse referring to this battle of Hunayn the Qur'an says: 'Then the very earth, in spite of its extent, seemed too small to provide a refuge for you when you turned your backs in flight' (Q9:25).

Muhammad, aged 60, was present in the valley and witnessed that panic moment 'when you turned your backs in flight'. Wearing his chain-mail coat and sitting astride a white mule, the Prophet stood his ground with his dedicated bodyguard surrounding him. 'Where are you going, men? I am the Messenger of God. I am the son of Abd al-Muttahib', he shouted above the noise.

Eventually a number of Muslim soldiers were persuaded by their leaders to turn and engage the Bani Hawazin in fierce hand-to-hand fighting. 'Now the oven is getting hot!' cried the Prophet. He was seen to lean forward eagerly to watch as the tide of the fighting ebbed and flowed. If a Bedouin tribe's fighting force did not break their enemy with that first wild charge they seldom lingered long, for they were usually after booty or honour, not death. In a short time the Hawazin broke away and ran for their lives.

Among the captives seized in the tents of the Bani Hawazin that had been pitched near to the battlefield was an old Bedouin woman of the Bani Sa'd who loudly claimed that she was the Prophet's sister. At first the Muslim soldiers merely laughed at her, but her persistence eventually won the day and two of them escorted her to Muhammad's distinctive tent, which was made of strips of leather dyed red. He came out to greet them. The old woman stepped forward.

'O Muhammad, I am your sister', she said simply. Notice that she used his first name. She exhibits here what you will find is one of the coloured threads woven into the carpet of this book, namely that peculiar mixture of affectionate respect and simple familiarity that is the charm of nomadic society.

'Have you any proof of that?' Muhammad asked her, for he did not recognize her by her face.

She replied by pulling up the sleeve of her dress to reveal the white scar of a bite mark on the brown skin. 'You gave me that,' she said, 'do you remember, one day when I was carrying you on my hip through the Wadi Sirhar to join the shepherds?'

The Bedouin captive was indeed Judama, his foster-sister. Muhammad was overcome with joy to see her again, and embraced her warmly. He spread his cloak for her in the time-honoured gesture and they sat down together. Until late into the evening they talked about their young days. Muhammad wanted to know about all that had befallen the members of his Bedouin foster-family. Next morning she was sent on her way back to the desert tents bearing gifts from Muhammad for herself and for her family.

When they heard Judama's story the chiefs of the Bani Sa'd clan of the Bani Hawazin saw their opportunity. They approached him and said: 'O Messenger of God, the women who suckled you as a baby and looked after you as a child are of our tribe. Have pity on us, the poor people who have suffered this disaster.'

'Which are dearest to you,' Muhammad asked, 'your children and your wives, or your flocks and herds?'

'Give us back our wives and children', they said to him as one.

According to the Bedouin *sunna*, after such a battle the captured women and children were never killed or otherwise harmed. But they did risk being sold into slavery, for they belonged among the spoils of victory, at least until the Caliph Umar issued a law prohibiting the sale of Arabs into slavery.

Muhammad undoubtedly had an obligation to grant the request of the Bani Sa'd chiefs, and he was scrupulous about such matters. But the Muslim warriors also expected to have their shares of the spoils of victory, which of course included the hapless Bani Sa'd men, women and children. Muhammad resolved the dilemma with considerable political acumen.

He told the Bani Sa'd chiefs to wait until a large assembly of the Muslim army's leaders had gathered for the noonday prayer.

'We ask the Messenger's intercession with the Muslims, and we ask for the Muslim's intercession with the Messenger to set free our wives and children!' cried out the Bani Sa'd chiefs in loud voices, following Muhammad's private instructions to the letter.

The soldiers from Medina spontaneously offered their share of the prisoners to the Prophet to dispose of as he pleased. But two of the Bedouin tribal contingents – the Fuzara and Bani Tamim – flatly refused to follow their example. So did the chief of a third tribe, the Bani Sulaym.

'Not so! What is ours belongs to the Messenger', declared the tribesmen of the Bani Sulaym, much to the chagrin of their sheikh.

The debate in the assembly between the Arabs, all free and equal in the discussion, raged hotly for an hour or more. Do not underestimate the difficulties of the situation. The Bedouin have a proverb: *The hawk dies with his eyes fixed on the prey*. Booty was the prey of the Bedouin, and they were as passionate about it as the hawk. Muhammad waited patiently for the right moment, and when it came he was ready with just the right compromise.

'Whoever insists on his right to a share of the prisoners should release them now and I will compensate him with six camels to every man from the next booty we take.'

Muhammad issued no orders. He told the men of the Bani Sa'd to appeal to the general assembly of the Muslims, using his practical wisdom to advise them correctly. He then showed judgement in choosing just the right time to exert his influence – for he knew the Bedouin well enough to know that six camels would prove more attractive to them than the burden of another wife! Notice too that he suggests to the Bani Sa'd leaders that they appeal to the Muslims to intercede with him – in other words, giving the Muslims the chance to gain honour in public by displaying their magnanimity. Muhammad knew the Arab nomads; after all he was, in Shakespeare's words, 'to the manner born'.

Another recipient of Muhammad's gifts after the battle of Hunayn was the young Bedouin *qaid* (Arabic: leader) Malik ibn Auf, who had hotly persuaded the Bani Hawazin chiefs to make war against the Muslims after the capture of Mecca. He had done so, incidentally, against the far wiser counsel of Durayd ibn al-Simma, the tribe's most senior chief.

Durayd was a veteran Bedouin war leader – the skin of his old legs, it is said, was as thin as paper from riding horses bareback on so many raids. Now, ailing in health, he conducted himself with the courage and dignity of a great Bedouin chief. To show that it was not cowardice – as some young hotheads had suggested – that had led him to oppose Malik's rash declaration of war against Muhammad, Durayd had himself taken to the battle in a camel litter. During the rout of the Hawazin, a young warrior of the Bani Sulaym, a Bedouin tribe fighting on the Muslim side, galloped up to the litter, seized the camel by the reins and thrust at him with his lance in a clumsy way.

'How badly has your mother reared you!' said Durayd, totally calm and self-possessed, and besides the Bedouin were remarkably unsentimental about death, their own or another's. Durayd then proceeded to give some advice to the beginner on how to kill him. 'There, take that sword hung up behind my litter, and strike just between the spine and the head. It was there I used to slay the adversary in my day. Then go and tell your mother that you have killed Durayd. Many are the days in which I have saved the lives of the women of your tribe.' He had indeed saved the youth's mother and his two grandmothers, but it earned him no mercy at Hunayn.

## KEY POINTS

- *A leader should exemplify or personify the qualities expected, required and admired in their working groups.* A leader of soldiers, for example, needs to demonstrate courage, 'the soldier's virtue', as Shakespeare called it.

- *Courage is a quality shown by Muhammad at Hunayn:* it is that which enables people to meet danger without giving way to fear, to act bravely under stress or to endure in times of adversity.

- *All members of working groups, organizations or communities – at all times in known history – share one thing in common:* they are all *persons* with a common and constant *human nature*.

- *A universal leader, then, will be a person who exemplifies such distinctively human qualities as goodness, kindness, humaneness and compassion.* Did you see any of these qualities in Muhammad?

- *Another generic quality of universal leaders is humility.* The word comes from the Latin root *humus* (ground, earth), related to *homo* (man). When Muhammad spread his cloak, lowered himself and sat on the ground with people at the same level, it was an act of humility. Compare a king sitting high upon a throne above his subjects, who abase themselves before him. As they will tell you in Ghana, 'Don't expect to be offered a chair when you visit a place where the chief himself sits on the floor.'

*It is the tribe that tells the chief how to do his job.*

ARAB PROVERB

# 2

# THE SHEPHERD

*'There is no prophet that has not worked as a shepherd,'*
*Muhammad used to say.*
*'Did you do so?' asked one present.*
*'Yes,' he replied. 'I herded sheep as a boy.'*

We do not know when the Prophet served as a shepherd, or for how long, or for whom he worked. But in retrospect Muhammad clearly saw this period as providential; it was almost, as he saw it, a necessary condition for being called as a prophet. It happened, of course, long before he knew that to be his destiny.

In this chapter I shall ask you to consider the possible lessons of leadership that Muhammad – as an intelligent and observant youth – might have gleaned from long days and nights shepherding a flock of sheep and goats in the wadis that threaded through the sun-baked hills and mountains around Mecca. Is that, I wonder, when he first came upon the cave where later, in about the year 610, he would come for weeks to be alone with God?

David was 30 years old when he began to reign over Israel, and he reigned 40 years. In the Qur'an he is called a prophet, as the authorship of the Book of Psalms is attributed to him. The Psalmist (78:70–72) summed up his vocation in these words:

*He chose David his servant,*
*And took him from the sheepfolds;*
*From tending the ewes that had young he brought him*
*To be the shepherd of Jacob his people, of Israel his*
*inheritance.*
*With upright heart he tended them,*
*And guided them with skilful hand.*

It is clear from this passage that probably the strongest ancient metaphor for a leader is that of the *shepherd*. Classical authors such as Homer and Xenophon had used the same image. Given our present knowledge of leadership it is a singularly rich image.

We know now that someone in a leadership role has three core and overlapping functions: to achieve the tasks, to hold a group together as a unity, and to meet individual needs. We know also that leadership is essentially a journey word. Putting these two insights together may help us to understand why the shepherd metaphor is so fertile in overtones and implications: it is a simple and serviceable model for a future leader, even though the lessons would have been more implicit than explicit.

The shepherd gave direction to the flock by leading it from the front, sometimes walking for up to 20 miles a day, in search of the sparse grass that grows in the wilderness. For even 'the pastures of the wilderness' (Psalm 65:12; John 2:22) were welcome in the spring, when the desert is green with fresh grass and flowers that will burn up in the summer heat. Lambs naturally follow their mothers, whilst fully grown wild sheep that live in bands follow their dominant ram.

To mark their paths, sheep have hoof-glands that give off scent. Early humans in the Mediterranean basin at least as long ago as 6000 BCE observed this phenomenon and saw that docile sheep could be tamed and induced to follow a human leader instead of a ram. Shepherds in the hill-country and in the wilderness had dogs, but the dogs were kept to protect the flocks of sheep and goats, and not used to round the flocks up or drive them.

As a rule, shepherds go before the flock, but not infrequently they are seen behind it. Shepherds walk behind, especially in the evening when the flock is on its way to the fold, in order that they may gather the stragglers and protect them from the stealthy wolf. Shepherds also often walk by the side of the flock, somewhere around the middle of the straggling line. In the case of large flocks the chief shepherd goes before, and the under-shepherd or helper brings up the rear. Keeping the flock close together was essential for its safety. No shepherd would go so far ahead as to lose sight or be out of earshot of the sheep. The natural instinct of predators, such as wolves and hyenas, was to scatter the flock and then kill their individual victims.

Therefore the unity or cohesiveness of the flock was important to shepherds. If they saw a sheep or goat wandering off, they called it back; should it still walk away, they hurled a stone from their sling, so as to fall just beyond it and send it scurrying back to the flock. If a sheep became lost 'on the hills' (Matthew 18:12), in the hills and gullies of the Judaean wilderness, the shepherd had to decide whether or not to leave the flock in order to go in search of it. If several shepherds had charge of the flock it was easier for one to go off, but even so the departure would weaken the collective strength of the shepherds, for the main threat to the flock came more from armed raiders rather than small mountain panthers or leopards, lions, bears, jackals, hyenas and wolves, which roamed in parts of Arabia in ancient times.

The shepherd, then, came to personify unity. Hence the proverb quoted by Jesus: *Smite the shepherd and the sheep will be scattered.* In order to keep their flocks safe and together at night, a time of greater danger, shepherds often herded them into the limestone caves that abound in the hills, or they made sheepfolds with drystone walls. In desert areas, where stones could not be found, they constructed their folds from thorn bushes. Wolves sometimes defied the dogs and leapt over these barriers, and so shepherds might keep some of the lambs and young kids close to their tent for the night. 'O fairest among women,' sings the author of the Song of Solomon (1:8), 'follow in the tracks of the flock, and pasture your kids beside the shepherds' tents.'

Flocks in Arab lands are often composed of sheep and goats, which are much more unruly than sheep alone. Goats tend to be black, while sheep in contrast are white, so they are easy to distinguish at a distance. Goats are especially fond of nibbling young leaves but will eat scrub, whereas sheep prefer the fresh short grass if they can find it. But sheep and goats in mixed flocks do not always coexist happily, and the shepherd must work to keep them together harmoniously. This characteristic made it often necessary to separate the goats from the sheep in the fold. In all human groups and organizations there are similar tendencies to internal divisiveness.

The perpetual journeys of shepherds and their flocks brought danger and hardship for all of them. The shepherds shared these dangers on an equal footing with the sheep. Shepherds carried no more than a bag or wallet, together with a staff and sling. The summer sun burnt shepherds and flocks by day, and all shivered in the winter snows and icy winds. Shepherds and sheep ran the risk of attacks by wild animals or of treading on deadly vipers that lurked in the limestone rocks. It is not hard to believe that the shepherds came to love their charges; each could be recognized individually and called by name. Therefore it is not surprising that the metaphor of the caring shepherd was applied to God. The 23rd Psalm is the song of an individual 'sheep', a person whose every need has been met by God the shepherd.

Like all analogies, the metaphor of the shepherd for a leader of people does break down eventually. People and sheep obviously differ in a number of important respects, but the broad functions of leadership are contained in the image. Shepherds respond to three kinds of implicit needs present in the flock: flocks need to find food, and so the shepherd leads them on the path to their desired destination; the shepherd holds them together in cohesive and harmonious unity; and, lastly, the shepherd meets their individual needs. Shepherds know each sheep or goat by name. They make sure that it finds the right food and enough water. They anoint an individual sheep's thorn-wounds with oil. They tend a sick animal until it recovers strength.

A joyful moment would come at sunset when the shepherd who had led out the flock of sheep in the morning brought them all safely back to the fold. It is one thing to lead people out on a journey, but it is another thing to bring them safely home. That analogy holds good for all forms of leadership. The successful military leader, for example, is the one who brings the army home in safety and, if it is victorious, in triumph, to a great welcome, with all the joys and celebrations of such a homecoming. For soldiers in all ages there is no sweeter experience.

Both Moses and David had worked as shepherds, and the implication is that some of the qualities and skills learnt there are transferable to the leadership of people and ultimately to the nation. David guided the human flock entrusted to him by God 'with skilful hand'. It is difficult not to believe that, in his youth, Jesus also had the care of the family's and neighbours' sheep and goats among the hills of Galilee, for the imagery of the shepherd informs his teaching on leadership. The Greek word for 'good' in the saying attributed to Jesus, 'I am the good shepherd' (John 10:14), is *kalos*, meaning skilful, as opposed to *agathos*, which means morally good. Good shepherd-leaders master the skills of leadership; they know their business. They are no hirelings who will run away at the first hint of danger; if need be, they will lay down their lives for the sheep entrusted to them.

The vision of a flock of sheep without a shepherd was the most powerful image in the ancient world for the need of a leader. On one of the very first clay tablets found – the world's earliest writing – was incised in cuneiform a Sumerian proverb: *Soldiers without a leader are like sheep without a shepherd*. It seems God calls a person to become a leader of a flock through the perception of the need for leadership. Moses had responded himself to that call to become the needed leader, and in due course he appointed as his successor Joshua, a man with the spirit in him as one 'who shall go out before them and come in before them, who shall lead them out and bring them in; that the congregation of the Lord may not be as sheep which have no shepherd' (Numbers 27:17).

One day when Muhammad was walking with others in the shade of the date palm trees in Medina, some boys passed him carrying some baskets of arak berries. Muhammad looked at his companions.

'Pick me out the blackest of them, for they are sweet', he said to them. 'Ones like that I used to gather when I fed the flocks of Mecca at Ajyad.'

They brought him the choicest of the fruit.

'Surely there has been no prophet raised up who did not do the work of a shepherd', said Muhammad once again, as if reflecting to himself.

## KEY POINTS

- *Leadership is done from in front.* In the human context a human leader may not always, on a physical journey, be the person out in front, just as the shepherd sometimes works behind the moving flock. But spiritually a leader is the one who leads from the front.

- *In leadership, example is everything.* As the Moorish proverb says: *When the shepherd is corrupt, so is his flock.*

- *Apart from leading the flock to pasture and water across the wilderness, shepherds have to keep the flock together and care for each individual sheep or lamb.* They will know the sheep by name, and the sheep in turn will know the shepherd's voice.

- *A good (Greek:* kalos, *skilled) shepherd meets on the level of the flock of sheep the three interactive circles of needs that are present in* **all** *human work groups at all times in history:* to achieve the common task, to be held together as a working unity, and the needs that individuals bring into the group by virtue of being individual embodied persons.

- *A good (Greek:* agathos, *morally good) shepherd is interested in the welfare of people, not in fleecing them.*

*When leaders are worthy of respect, the people are willing to work for them. When their virtue is worthy of admiration, their authority can be established.*

HUANANZI (CHINESE PHILOSOPHER, 4TH CENTURY BC)

# 3

# CARAVAN LEADER

*When travelling on a journey, even if there are only three of you, make one a leader.*

MUHAMMAD

The Quraysh – Muhammad's tribe – were once part of a larger confederation of tribes in the Najd desert known as the Bani Kinana. As with other Bedouin tribes it had been their custom from time immemorial to join the annual *hajj* (Arabic: pilgrimage) to a barren valley between jagged arid mountains where a sacred spring called Zamzam brought its cold, clear water to the surface. Nearby stood an unusual standing stone – black meteorite – that the ancestors of the Bedouin may have worshipped once as a god. In Muhammad's day they would touch or kiss the venerated Black Stone (Arabic: *Al-Hajar al-aswad*) before sacrificing an animal.

In the course of time this holy place came to be known in Arabic as Mecca. The form of that word used by Ptolemy (*c*90–168 CE) – *Macoraba* – gives us its meaning, for in several Semitic languages it signifies a temple. We think of a temple as a large building in the Egyptian or Graeco-

Roman form, but a temple in the early Semitic context is simply an enclosure: a low wall made of stones or rocks around a holy site, initially built to keep stray animals away. The Black Stone was eventually protected – probably for the same reason – by the *al-Ka'ba* (Arabic: the cube).

Qusay was a chief of the Quraysh. While they still lived in the desert, he happened to marry the daughter of a chief of the Bani Khuzan tribe who had installed himself as the guardian of the temple at Mecca. On his father-in-law's death, aided by his Bani Kinana kinsmen from the desert, Qusay overcame his Khuzan rivals and took charge of Mecca. The Khuzan were driven out. Packing their tents on to their camels they returned to the nomadic life in the Najd from whence they had come.

It was Qusay who built the first stone dwelling house around the temple enclosure and began to manage the annual pilgrimage partly for profit. He levied a tax on his fellow tribesmen to support poor or needy pilgrims, which doubtless brought him great prestige among the desert tribes, who so much valued generous hospitality. Muhammad's grandfather Abd al-Muttahib, who had looked after him for two years when he was orphaned, was a great-grandson of Qusay. Here is his noble message to his fellow tribesmen:

'You are God's neighbour, the people of his temple and sanctuary. The pilgrims are God's guests and visitors to his temple, and they have the highest claim on your generosity, so provide food and drink for them during their pilgrimage until they depart out of your territory.'

With their institution of a ban on all warfare and violence in the region around Mecca during the annual pilgrimages, the Quraysh also in effect gave their protection to the devout wayfarers who converged in large crowds on the holy place.

Mecca was one of a number of small commercial and agricultural towns in the hilly areas of the Hejaz in western Arabia. There were settled communities, too, in the great date-growing oases of Yemen on the Gulf coast. Most of these towns and markets were mainly used for the exchange of the wool and leather of the pastoralists, and for the grain, olive oil and wine that were the main luxuries. From about 500, however, the mining of precious metals in the Hejaz added a new dimension. Some of the mines were owned and operated by Bedouin tribes like the Bani Sulaym. The production of precious metals greatly increased the prosperity of the area. At least some of the Bedouin tribes now had the means to become important consumers of the produce of the settled lands. Groups of merchants emerged to import goods from Syria, setting up networks between the tribes to allow their caravans to pass in peace.

As the decades passed, the settled Arabs, the occupants of the small towns and villages that grew up around a well or oasis (Arabia has no rivers), became more distinct from their Bedouin cousins, the desert nomads. They prided themselves on the virtue of *hilm*, that included such qualities as gentleness, clemency, mildness and forebearance. They considered the Bedouin tribes to be excitable and unreliable, useful for their military skills in desert warfare and for their hardiness but needing to be controlled and led. For their part many of the Bedouin tribal chiefs – without surrendering any of their essential freedom and independence – proved to be willing to accept the leadership of the high-status tribes in the towns, such as the Quraysh in Mecca and the Thaqif in nearby Taif, when occasion demanded it.

A modern example of the same principle arose in the First World War, when the Sharif of Mecca and his four sons – direct descendants of the Prophet and of Muhammad's clan in the Quraysh, the Hashemites – led the Arab

Revolt against their Turkish overlords, supported and largely funded by their British and French allies. The Sharifian army under Faisal, which entered Damascus in 1918, consisted of a small force of Arab soldiers drawn from the towns – mostly deserters from the Turkish army – and a much more numerous horde of Bedouin tribesmen recruited from the different tribes along the road to Damascus. For example, the famous chief of the Bani Howeitat, Auda abu Tayi – whom we shall meet again in the next chapter – led his tribesmen in the capture of the port of Akaba, the turning point of the campaign. And the survival of one of those sons, Abdullah, and his son Hussein, as King of Jordan depended more than once upon that ancient willingness of the Bedouin tribes to give their personal loyalty to leaders descended from the Prophet's tribe.

Muhammad revered his grandfather. You may recall that at the battle of Hunain in the Arab manner he shouted out as his personal war cry: 'I am Muhammad, son of Abd al-Muttahib!' Abd al-Muttahib was a chief or *shaykh* in the great tradition, one who personified the virtues that Arabs valued and expected in their leaders. One of the poets commissioned to compose and recite eulogies in his honour sang of him:

*Alas, has the shepherd of his people, the generous one, perished,*
*Who gave the pilgrims their water, the defender of our fame,*
*Who used to carry the wandering guest into his tents,*
*When the heavens begrudged their rain.*

Notice that image of 'the shepherd of his people', returning here like a musical refrain. Did Muhammad as a boy dream of being such a shepherd?

Thanks to long-standing quarrels between the various kinship groups and lineages, the Quraysh had no acknowledged single tribal chief. In that respect perhaps they could be seen as a flock without a shepherd. This lack of strong leadership, however, would work to Muhammad's advantage later on, when the Quraysh lacked a leader of sufficient stature and wisdom to deal with the man who became the thorn in their side.

By a set of complex established precedents the leading Qurayshi families shared between them the functions of leadership. They divided up such responsibilities as the guardianship of the temple, the maintenance of the house of meeting that stood near the enclosure, the right to carry the tribal banner in battle, the collection of the charitable tax to provide hospitality and succour for the poorest pilgrims, and the arranging of the divinations that took place before the idols of the various tribal gods such as Hubal that now also stood within the large sacred enclosure.

Decisions of importance were made by the heads of lineages by reaching consensus in the time-honoured manner of the Bedouin *majlis* (Arabic: place of sitting, from *jalasa*, to be seated). With its sides open to the winds their one-storey 'house of meeting' next to the temple was simply a Bedouin chief's tent of meeting made out of stone.

Under Islam much later a *majlis* came to mean a public audience granted by a ruler such as a caliph, sultan or emir. But it retained its sense as a public forum for the conduct of political matters or legal judgements, what in English would come to be called a *parliament* (from the French *parler*, to speak; the original sense of the word was the action of speaking, speech, conference or discussion: hence the council called by a monarch to discuss some matter of general importance).

Without any police force at his disposal a chief depended upon his personal authority – the strength of his personality and the wisdom of his judgements – to lead where he could not command. Charles Doughty, the 19th-century English traveller in Arabia, once described in his distinctive prose style the *majlis* of Shaykh Mutlaq, the chief of the Fugara tribe:

> *When the majlis assembled numerous at his tent, he, the great shaykh and host, would sit out with a proud humility among the common people, holding still his looks at the ground; but they were full of unquiet sideglances, as his mind was erect and watching. His authority slumbered till, there being some just occasion, he ruled with a word the unruly Bedu… The shaykh of a nomad tribe is no tyrant; a great shaykh striking a tribesman he should bruise his own honour.*

In fact guiding such a meeting to an actionable decision required not only the authority of position and personal prestige but also skill. Do you imagine Muhammad as a boy ever sitting on the edge of the open-sided meeting house in order to learn that skill? I do.

A more modern tribal example may illustrate that possibility. Nelson Mandela's father – a chief of the Thembu tribe – used to take him as a young boy to the Great Place, where the paramount chief Mohekezweni used to discuss tribal issues with tribal chiefs and any Thembus who wished to attend. The leader of leaders was surrounded by his councillors. Mandela later recalled:

*My later notions of leadership were profoundly influenced by observing the paramount chief... I watched and learned from the tribal meetings that were regularly held at the Great Place and as a leader I have always followed the principles I first saw demonstrated there.*

*I have always endeavoured to listen to what each and every person in a discussion had to say before venturing my own opinion. Oftentimes my own opinion will simply represent a consensus of what I heard in the discussion.*

Maybe when he was 14, Muhammad was present at the *majlis* when the Quraysh chiefs decided to join in a war that had erupted in the desert. Some Bani Hawazin tribesmen had raided a caravan near Mecca and killed the guide. He came from the Bani Kinana, and the caravan was under that tribe's protection. To make matters worse this fatal assault took place in the month before the great annual pilgrimage to Mecca, when any violence in the environs of the town was strictly forbidden. Consequently a war broke out between the two tribes that lasted five years, and it is not difficult to guess what side the Meccans were on. Muhammad accompanied his uncles in the Meccan contingent to one battle, and it is said that he made himself useful by picking up spent arrows on the field afterwards.

This story illustrates how the Meccans could not have isolated themselves from desert politics even if they had wanted to do so. And there would be no better way for Muhammad to get to know desert politics than by becoming a caravan leader. And it is speculation on my part – no more – that as a young man he may well have done so.

The Quraysh were in the business of caravans for they were merchants; they carried on trade on a large scale with Syria in the north and Yemen in the south. Their caravans to and from Damascus had to complete a journey of a thousand miles. They carried among other things dyed and finely worked leather goods made from skins obtained from the Bedouin tribes, often at the great fairs held at pilgrimage time.

Every large caravan was headed by a *qaid* (pronounced 'akide'). In Arabic that word could be applied to a guide, the leader of a raid on another tribe's camels, or a military commander. The commander of the Bedouin regiment of the Arab Legion in which I served when I was 20 had that title.

*Qiyada*, leadership (Arabic has no infinitive), derives from the Arab word *yaqud*, meaning 'he leads'. A derivative is *miqwad* – a rope that is used to lead a horse or camel by the head. Strictly speaking, however, no one in Arabian society would presume to call themselves a *qa'id* or leader. Originally, at any rate, it was more like an accolade or compliment. The same applies, incidentally, to *leader* in English.

It is interesting to see how close the Arabic and English languages are at this point. Meaning a road, way, path or course of a ship at sea, the Anglo-Saxon word *laed* is the root of the English words *leader, leadership* and *to lead*. It is related to the verb *laedan*, to go or travel, or, in its causative form, to make or cause to go. In fact it is a North European root, with similar-sounding equivalents in old Norse, German and Dutch. Clearly leadership is a journey concept. A leader, literally, is one who leads the way by going first, the one, too, who may cause or make others to go on a journey and holds them together in a body so that they do not get out of touch or lose their unity as a body – remember the shepherd!

The -*ship* ending of leadership derives from the Anglo-Saxon verb 'to shape'. Known as a suffix in English, the -*ship* word ending has two distinct meanings, and that can be a bit confusing. Here it can mean: 1) an office, dignity or position of a leader; or 2) the qualities or attributes of being a leader. The distinction becomes clearer when it is observed that not all those who occupy roles or positions of leadership – by birth, election or appointment – have the personal ability and knowledge of how to lead. Plutarch, for example, described a Roman emperor named Gaius Antonius as 'a man with no aptitude for leadership in any direction, either good or bad'. The Africans have a proverb to describe such a ruler: *A log of wood may lie in the river for years but it never becomes a crocodile.*

'You can be appointed a commander or manager,' it has been said, 'but you are not a leader until your appointment is ratified in the hearts and minds of those you lead.' Perhaps it was while leading caravans that Muhammad discovered that he had a natural gift for leadership. What do you think?

The role of a caravan leader was an exceptionally responsible one. Before the caravan left Mecca, for example, a hundred or more camels and camel-drivers had to be selected and hired, the loads assembled and packed for the camels, provisions and tents bought and loaded, weapons prepared, and money secured for expenses en route and for the wages of the camel-drivers.

Once out in the desert on the tracks leading north, all accountability for the caravan rested solely on the shoulders of the caravan leader. He was without any means of communication with the owners once Mecca had receded from sight. Nor was the caravan insured. If any property in his care was damaged or stolen, it was the caravan leader and his kinsfolk who were obliged to recompense the owners.

The Bedouin tribes made part of their money by extracting protection money from caravans that passed through their territory. Therefore a key function of a caravan leader was negotiating with the right tribe for the right amount of money or goods. The desert nomads respected noble lineage. Therefore the best guarantee for the security of a caravan as it plodded its way through the wilderness was the personal prestige of its chosen leader, and the respect engendered by the fact that he was a member of a distinguished family in Mecca. As you would expect, the *qaid* of a caravan always accompanied it in person.

The Greek Byzantines in Muhammad's day called a caravan leader a *synodiarch*. The word literally means a 'chief, ruler or leader of a meeting or council'. In Palmyra, a great oasis and city in northern Arabia, a group of Palmyrene merchants erected a monument in 193 CE to a caravan leader who had won their gratitude. The inscription reads:

*'This statue is in honour of Taymarsu, chief of the caravan [synodiarch], which has been made for him by members of the caravan who came up with him from Charax, because he paid their expenses, three hundred gold coins in ancient currency, and was well pleasing to them...'*

'On a journey', Muhammad once said, 'the leader of a people is their servant.' What did he mean? That a true leader *serves* those whom he or she leads, both as a *group* – meeting their needs to complete their journey safely and their needs to be maintained as a cohesive whole – and also as a set of *individuals*, for each *individual* on a journey may have small needs or problems as the journey proceeds. Would you like to see Muhammad as a servant-leader in action? Fortunately we can.

Wahb ibn Kaysan once accompanied Muhammad on a raid. When they set out from Medina he was riding an old feeble camel. It is he who tells the following story:

*On the way back the company kept going on while I dropped farther behind until the apostle overtook me and asked me what the trouble was. I told him that my camel was keeping me back, and he told me to make it kneel. I did so and the apostle made his camel kneel.*

*'Give me this stick you are holding' or 'Cut a stick from a tree', he said [Wahb could not quite remember which]. He took it and prodded the beast with it a few times. Then he told me mount and off we went. By Him who sent him with the truth my (old) camel kept us up with the rapid pace of his she-camel.*

*As we were talking, the apostle asked me if I would sell him my camel. I said that I would give him it, but he insisted on buying it, so I asked him to make me an offer. He said he would give me a dirham. I refused and said that would be cheating me. Then he offered two dirhams and I still refused and the apostle went on raising his offer until it amounted to an ounce (of gold). When I asked him if he was really satisfied he said that he was and I said the camel was his.*

*Then he asked me if I were married; then was she a virgin or a woman previously married? I told him she had been married before. 'No girl so that you could sport together!' he said. I told him that my father had been killed at Uhud leaving seven daughters and I had married a motherly woman who could look after them efficiently.*

*'You have done well, if God will', he said. 'Had we come to Sirar [a place about three miles from Medina] we would order camels to be slaughtered and stay there for the day and she would hear about us and shake the dust off her cushions.'*

*'But by God we have no cushions!' I replied.*

*'But you will have', the Prophet said, and added: 'When you return behave wisely.'*

*When we got to Sirar the apostle ordered the camels to be slaughtered and we stayed there for the day. At night the apostle went home and so did we. I told the woman the news and what the apostle had said to me.*

*'Look alive and do what he tells you.' In the morning I led away the camel and made it kneel at the apostle's door. Then I sat inside the mosque hard by. He came out and saw it and asked what it was, and they told him it was the camel which I had brought. He asked where I was and I was summoned to him.*

*'O son of my brother,' he said, 'take away your camel for it is yours.' And he called Bilal and told him to give me an ounce of gold.*

Bilal was a former slave whom Muhammad had appointed as the first muezzin (the person appointed to call Muslims to prayer). He gave Wahb the ounce of gold, and Muhammad added a little more gold to it.

What is remarkable about this story is first that the Prophet Muhammad noticed the young man struggling on the old camel and stopped to help him. He enjoyed playfully haggling for the camel, which he had no intention of buying, and in the process finding out more about Wahb. As the son of a fallen hero at Uhud – 'son of my brother' – he was a worthy recipient of the generous gift that ends the story. Muhammad has behaved as a great Arab chief should, but with a characteristically gentle and humorous touch.

## KEY POINTS

- *Muhammad looked up to his grandfather Abd al-Muttahib, briefly his father as well.* He personified what the Arabs called *muruwwa*, the virtue of being a man. It connotes a cluster of virtues: bravery, generosity, practical wisdom and honour, all highly valued and praised in Arab tribal culture. These are the qualities we see in Muhammad.

- *Practical wisdom – the Greeks called it* phronesis *– is essentially the art of knowing the right thing to do at the right time and in the right away.* It encompasses the ability to see ahead, to predict how things will unfold, and also to forecast what will be the consequences of a given course of action.

- *Being a caravan leader – being a leader in any context – calls for such judgement or practical wisdom:* the ability to come to sound conclusions, to make wise decisions based upon them, and to act upon them with decisiveness and determination.

- *No one is born wise; a leader becomes wise – acquires practical wisdom – through natural aptitude, practice and reflection.* Wisdom, like an Arab bow made of different kinds of wood, has three elements: *intelligence*, *experience* and *goodness*.

- *The caravan leader is not the caravan's official guide, or* dalil, *who piloted the camel train through his knowledge of the landmarks.* The *qaid* fulfilled the generic or universal role of *leader*: achieving the task successfully, maintaining group coherence or unity, and caring for individual members.

- *Meeting these three areas of interactive or overlapping need called for skill, but it was best performed in a spirit of* service. Serve to lead. Muhammad learnt that great lesson. For an example of the humble service he rendered to a companion on a journey when he was the leader, see above.

*On a journey the leader of a people is their servant.*

MUHAMMAD

# 4

# Dwellers of the
# **DESERT**

*If you show a Bedouin
the entrance to your house,
then open wide the door
that his camel may enter.*

ARAB PROVERB

*'Are there camels in heaven?' an anxious Bedouin asked
the Prophet.*

According to one early Muslim writer, an Arab skilled
in oratory was sent in 531 CE to the court of the great
Persian emperor Khosro (Chosroes I), who had expressed
curiosity about his people and in particular why the
Bedouin tribes chose to live without the protection of
walled cities in their desert homelands.

*'O king,' replied the Arab, 'they are masters of their land
rather than mastered by it, and they have no need for*

*fortification walls, since they can rely on sharp sword blades and pointed lances for their protection and defence.'*

*'What is the Arab's main sustenance?' Khosro then asked.*

*'Meat, milk, date-wine and dates', replied the envoy.*

*'And what are their qualities?' Khosro wanted to know next.*

*'Courage, honour, magnanimity, extending hospitality to the guest, providing security to the client, granting refuge to the weak, repaying favours and dispensing generosity', said the Arab with a poet's gift for words and phrases.*

*'They are travellers of the stealthy raid,' he continued, 'dwellers of the desert, the good hosts of the wilderness. They are accustomed to self-restraint in eating and drinking and averse to subordination or obsequious cringing. They practise vengeance, abhor disgrace or shame, and do everything in their power to preserve their honour.'*

All the essential ingredients of the contemporary Arab character and way of life are captured in this story, not least the eloquence of the Arab spokesman at its centre. Notice that the Arabs – all Arabs – are identified as 'dwellers of the desert'. In fact the language is Arabic and the land Arabia simply because the desert nomads called themselves *arab* or 'the Arab people' from time immemorial and were known as such by their neighbours. Later, as the distinction between nomads and settlers became more pronounced, the nomads who adhered to their desert life as pastoralists became known in Arabic as *badawi*, from *badw*, the great barren wilderness of rock, gravel and sand where they lived and roamed with their flocks of camels and sheep. There are various spellings for *badawi*, but the current one in English I have used in this book is *Bedouin*, which can function as both singular and plural. In the period roughly between the Byzantine era and the end of the Crusades the nomadic people of the deserts of Syria and Arabia – and more broadly the Arabs as a whole – were also known as Saracens (possibly from *sharqi* Arabic: sunrise, east, and *sharqiyyin*, easterners – in the biblical Book of Judges the nomads are called 'the sons of the east'). But, as I have said, they called themselves *arab*.

For more than three thousand years before Muhammad, the Arabs were a people of the one-humped camel. The Assyrian king Esarhaddon in 671 BCE, for example, recorded on stone: 'Camels of all the kings of the Arab I gathered and waterskins I loaded on them.' Thus provided he was able to transport his army over the Syrian desert in order to attack Egypt. In their later days the Persian rulers Cambyses and Ataxerses both followed his example, and assembled caravans of camels in their thousands. If it is not worked too hard and has good grazing a camel can get all the water it needs from the moisture in its food, and go without a proper drink for as long as 10 months. In emergencies it can take what water it needs directly from its own body tissues, losing up to a quarter of its body weight without being seriously weakened. With a load of 500 pounds (227 kilograms), a camel can cover 25 miles a day for three days in a row. Unloaded, it can run 10 miles an hour for 18 hours at a stretch, jog-trot at five miles an hour for 24 hours, or pad along at a walk for days.

For the rider – as I can testify – the long hours of slow movement swaying in the wooden-framed saddle covered with leather and woven trappings can be a real test of endurance. After becoming weary in the saddle as the sun goes down and the desert begins to lose its colours, one longs to catch sight of some black tents with their welcoming call of hospitality, a blazing fire of fragrant wood, coffee and food and a bed for the night under the canopy of bright stars.

A female riding camel that is loath to part from her young or herd moans grievously, for several days. But often the murmuring lasts for months. Day after day, and often at night as well, the rolling murmur is heard at regular intervals. It will not cease unless the animal's mouth is tied with a cord, but even then a subdued sound is still heard. The Semitic word for the camel's passionate maternal love occurs again in Biblical Hebrew for God's yearning love for humankind.

For Muhammad the camel was not only 'God's gift', (Q88: 17–22), to the Arabs but also one of the wonders of creation that invite us to believe in a wise and good creator:

*Will they not consider the camels, how they are made,*
*The sky, how it is raised high?*
*And the mountains, how they are fixed firm?*
*And the earth, how it is spread out?*

Q88:17–20

Well, have *you* ever considered how the camel is made? In fact everything about the camel is designed to fit it for the relentless heat and aridity of Arabia. The eyes – to a non-Arab about the only beautiful feature – are double-lashed in a heavy fringe that screens out the stinging grains of sand in a sandstorm. The ears and nostrils can be closed up tight for the same purpose. The feet, disproportionately large at the bottom of skinny shins, are splayed and padded to move over sand without sinking.

As for eating, the camel's tough lips can nibble at spiky thorns, and are so good at gathering food that it never has to lose precious moisture by sticking its tongue out. Indeed, camels will devour things that few other living creatures would look at twice – desert salt-bush or sun-baked acacia leaves. This 'food' is moved back and forth through four stomach chambers, which extract nourishment from the unlikeliest sources with very little waste. One result of this thorough processing is exceptionally dry dung, which burns beautifully when used as fuel for cooking a nomad dinner.

The camel's most legendary feature is its minimal need for water. Although the dromedary (from the Greek *dromas kamelos*, running camel) does need watering in the hot summer it can survive on the moisture in vegetation in winter when a few inches of rain fall on the steppes. Unlike most animals that are poisoned if they do not urinate enough to expel waste urea, the camel can recycle much of its urea through the liver to make new protein, thereby keeping ahead on both food and water.

Bedouin use camel urine, which smells sweetly of aromatic plants, to wash their hair and keep it black and shiny – it helps to destroy parasites. The father of a newborn baby may run out of his tent, kick his camel to make it rise and massage its right flank to induce it to urinate. His wife would then bathe the infant all over, as if baptizing the baby with this herb-scented water of the beast of the desert.

Camel's milk was often the nomad's only food. Every day a she-camel can give her owner a gallon of milk much richer than a cow's, and she will provide it for at least three years after bearing a calf. When he lived in Medina, Muhammad owned a herd of camels on the fringe of the oasis. It included one each for his wives so that they had a daily supply of milk. Umm Salma, one of his wives, recalled:

*Our chief food when we lived with Muhammad was milk. The camels used to be brought from Al Ghaba every evening. I had one called Aris, and Aisha one called al-Samra. The herdsman fed them at al-Juania and brought them to our homes in the evening. There was one for Muhammad.*

*Hind and Asman, two herdsmen, used to feed them, one day at Uhud, the other at Himna. They beat down leaves from the wild trees for them, and on these the camels fed during the night. They were milked for the guests of the Prophet, and his family got what was over. If the evening drew in and the camel's milk was late in being brought, Muhammad would say: 'The Lord make thirsty him who makes thirsty the family of Muhammad at night.'*

The fact that this herd of camels belonged to the Messenger and Prophet of God did not protect them from Bedouin raiders. On at least one occasion Muhammad accompanied the party that set out in pursuit of the raiders in order to recover his beloved camels. Indeed Muhammad had no time for those who did not take proper care of their camels. An Arab once came to Muhammad to see if he had a prophet's or seer's gift of knowing the location of a stray camel. The Arab had recently lost his camel, he explained to the Prophet, and it was wandering about somewhere in the desert. But he had come to the wrong prophet. Muhammad never claimed the particular gift of being able to find lost animals by a miraculous second sight. And so instead of directions for finding the missing animal, the Arab owner received some pointed but practical advice:

*'Why did you not tie back the camel's knee?' asked the Prophet.*

*'I did not tie it,' the Arab replied, 'because I put my trust in God.'*

*'Both tie and trust', the Prophet told him.*

To the Arab nomads camels were their principal wealth and means of exchange. The bride-price for a wife, for example, would be paid for in camels. They were also symbols of honour and pride, so that in battle a warrior might include among his war cries the names of his camels after those of his father, son or sister. And in the constant intertribal raids and wars the camels of the enemy were always the principal object.

To the practised Bedouin eye, nothing was as useful or beautiful as a fine riding female camel. There were over 300 names for different colours, shapes and sizes of camel in Arabic. For example, a *rhasa* is a camel in whose hoof either a thorn or a sharp stone has stuck. *Hadijja* is the term applied to a she-camel that grazes only near her resting rider and will not go far enough to lose sight of the rider. It is no accident that the Arabic words *jamal* (camel) and *jamil* (beautiful) come from the same root.

As a riding camel has a life span of about 40 years, a considerable bond of mutual attachment could develop between an owner and the beast. The passion that a Bedouin could feel towards a chosen camel is well conveyed in a scene that a traveller, Carl Raswan, a German officer with the Turks in the First World War but by then an American, witnessed when he was living with the great Bedouin tribe the Ruwalla in the Syrian desert in the 1920s.

A tribesman of the Bani Sakhr had been mortally wounded in a raid, and Raswan had a medical kit with him, but he could do nothing beyond trying to alleviate the man's pain. Raswan's graphic account in *The Black Tents of Arabia* (1926) speaks volumes about Bedouin values and their way of life:

*Friends carried him presently the short distance to Ibn Jeneyb's tent and laid him down there. Then a slave led up a handsome riding-camel. It was touching to see how the intelligent animal seemed to sense that its master was dying. It caressed him repeatedly, and with large, anxious eyes circled round, touching the strange men with its slit lips and its soft silky nostrils. The dying man was speaking to Ibn Jeneyb, his chieftain, when a severe haemorrhage caused him to faint. When he came to again, he whispered some words to the slave; and before I could take in what was happening, the slave, bending back the camel's head, killed it with a lightning plunge of his dagger into the jugular vein.*

*Other slaves immediately skinned the animal and spread out the hide, the bloody side up, before the tent. Then they undressed the dying man and laid him on it. His last wish had been to be buried in the skin of his cherished dhalul (riding camel), and the thought that his wish was to be realized made him happy as he lay dying. But I was not the only one to regret the purposeless death of the splendid animal.*

*When, toward evening the man had breathed his last, four or five of the watchers, his friends, got up one after another and lightly touched his forehead with their finger-tips. Ibn Jeneyb, who knelt beside the dead man, put his hand under his left armpit; after a while he called out: 'In truth, he is cold!'*

*Getting up hastily, he folded the wet, bloody winding-sheet over the corpse and directed his slaves to dig a grave for him in the sand. Without ceremony or any show of emotion it was borne away and given into the keeping of the earth.*

This story could have taken place in the lifetime of Muhammad.

When Muhammad left Mecca in 622 CE to ride to Medina, some 350 kilometres to the north, he bought a camel called *al-Qaswaa* from Abu Bakr, a beast that would be close to his heart until his death. He also owned a riding camel called *Adhba*, so swift that Muhammad believed it to be the best. But one day at a full gallop a Bedouin overtook and passed him. 'It is the nature of God', said Muhammad to him with a smile afterwards, 'that whenever men exalt anything or seek to do so then He puts down the same.'

When Harun al-Rashid of the 'Abbasid dynasty was caliph in Baghdad (786–809), one night he entertained a visiting Arab poet called Asma'i. He told the court historian Marzubani what ensued:

*Al-Rashid asked me if I knew the poem of 'Adi ibn Riqa' with the line 'He knew the dwellings instinctively and visited them repeatedly.' I replied 'yes' and he said 'go ahead then'.*

*So I started reciting it until I got to where he describes his camel, when Fadl ibn Yahya al-Barmaki [a Persian courtier] exclaimed: 'I beseech you by God not to interrupt our enjoyment of this nightly gathering of ours by describing a scabby camel.'*

*'Keep quiet!' said al-Rashid. 'It is the camels who have driven you Persians from your home and power, taking away the crown of your kingship.'*

The *ghazw* (Arabic: raiding) – sudden, hostile incursions into another tribe's territory to seize camels – was integral to the Arab way of life. When a *qa'id* or leader proposed such a raid it was left to each man to volunteer. Each Bedouin was free to go or stay. Each brought his own camel, weapons, goatskin of water and saddle-bags of provisions. Given a tried and trusted leader there was usually no shortage of volunteers, for raiding was a part of their life. A good leader was one who was courageous, capable and known for his luck.

In the fighting – be it a short and sharp raid on the other tribe's herds or (if the parties were not even distantly related) on their encampment – the *qa'id* was expected to lead from in front. The raiding party rode to the scene of the attack on she-camels, sometimes two men to a camel. If they had horses and the distances were not too great, horses would be led behind the camels and mounted for the fight.

His knowledge of the Bedouin ways was extremely useful to Muhammad as a leader during the desert war between the Muslims and the Quraysh. When the Quraysh were marching southwards after their victory at the battle of Uhud, the weary Muslim commanders on the high ground of the ridge watched anxiously to see if they would turn aside and attack the settlements in the oasis of Medina as they passed by or continue home to Mecca with their spoils. Muhammad asked the most keen-sighted among them: 'Are they riding camels and leading horses, or riding horses and leading camels?' When informed that the Quraysh were mounted on their camels he then concluded correctly that they were bound for Mecca.

Arab poets have left us glowing descriptions of successful raids, but in reality things could be very different. In 1921, for example, the fame of Auda abu Tayi of the Bani Howeitat tribe as a *qa'id* of raiding parties attracted 120 men drawn from several tribes to gather at a rendezvous east of Ma'ar (in what is now Jordan). Auda's intention was to raid the camel flocks of some Iraqi tribes who were camped on the western bank of the Euphrates, north-west of Baghdad, about 600 kilometres away from the starting point.

Things began to go wrong when the raid approached its objective. A single camel rider, probably a scout, was seen to be observing them from afar, and he outran those sent in his pursuit. Once the alarm had been raised and the opportunity for surprise had been lost the raiders had little chance of success. The grazing flocks would be driven back hurriedly to the camps of their owners, while the fighting men of the tribes mustered to repel the invaders. And so the raiders decided to abandon the enterprise and they turned for home.

Desperately short of water, as the wells they had planned to use were guarded, they set out for a waterhole that lay three days' march further to the west. It was very risky because, if they did not find water at the hole they had in mind, there was no other supply for another 200 kilometres. When they got to the waterhole, their worst fear was confirmed: it was dry. Disaster now stared them in the face. Discipline, never strong among the nomads, broke down.

'I thought that you were a famous raider', said one young sheikh insolently to Auda. 'You have not done very well this time, have you?' he added. 'First we miss our booty and now we look like dying of thirst!' Other tribesmen murmured their support of the rebel.

Auda's fierce face had gone livid with rage, and his hand had reached towards his rifle, which was lying by his side.

'You may not live long enough to die of thirst, cursed one!' he replied through clenched teeth. Having killed, it was reputed, over 300 men in battle – 'not counting Turks', he once added – Auda was quite capable of carrying out his threat.

'For God's sake, do not start a fight here!' cried his son Mohamed, seizing his father's wrist. 'We can have it out with them when we get home – if any of us ever get back.'

'Very well, I quit the leadership', announced Auda, having struggled to master his fury. 'You may all go your own ways, and may a curse go with you!'

Only 25 men from the Bani Howeitat followed Auda as they started a desperate ride for the nearest water to the west. They forced the pace unmercifully, marching all night, so as to avoid the loss of moisture caused by effort in the heat, snatching short sleeps in the middle of the day. Drinking had been reduced to a mere cupful a day, or less, and, without adequate water, food had become inedible. All spare kit, arms and ammunition had been jettisoned to reduce weight, but camels soon started to fail. As a mount dropped out, it had been killed and ripped open so that its storage stomach could be squeezed dry of its reserve of water.

Some of the men were driven by desperation to drinking camel's blood. This had fatal results, as in every case the drinkers eventually collapsed in delirium. As a camel was killed, the rider doubled up with another man. When there was no more room, the riders of dead camels were abandoned to certain death under the glaring sun of a waterless and featureless desert. Once or twice, as the survivors rode on without a word of farewell or backward glance, they heard the dry crack of the rifle shot with which the sufferer had put himself out of misery.

After finishing his share of water, Mohamed had ridden for twenty-four hours without a drink. He had then been overcome by faintness and had told his father he could go no further. Auda had looked at his son with haggard eyes and had muttered through cracked and bleeding lips, 'Hang on until dark. God is merciful.' He would offer no further explanation. Somehow or other, Mohamed had found a last reserve of strength and had struggled on until nightfall; then his father had taken him aside and had produced an army water bottle that he had carried hidden in his saddle wraps. They had had a mouthful of water each and the precious bottle had gone back to its hiding-place until the following night.

The nightmare ride had come to an end at a well in the northern end of the Wadi Sirhan. The survivors, 10 men with ravaged faces and staring eyes, fell off their camels and drank the water of life.

Horses were few in number in Arabia but highly valued for their use in raiding or warfare generally. The pure-bred Arabian was smaller, leaner and more finely hewn than its Western counterparts. A true Arab horse has a unique gait when galloping, as if it literally hovers over the ground. As the Arab proverb says, *God created the first man from earth but he made the horse out of the sky.*

Arabia is without rivers or meadows, and, unlike camels, horses cannot survive on thorns. They need water and proper feeding. Yet the Bedouins' application of their phenomenal memory for genealogy, together with the care they lavished on their horses, made them the greatest horse-breeders of their day. Just three Arab stallions imported from Arabia by English breeders in the 19th century are the ancestors of all the thoroughbred horses in the world today.

According to the Arabs, one of the highest gifts of God to man on earth, or in the world to come, is the companionship of an Arabian horse. The early Arab historian Ibn Hisham (died 827 CE) remembered that as a boy his father had told him: 'Ishmael, son of Abraham, was the first human being to ride a horse and the first to speak Arabic (the language of the angels), and the first to shoot from the bow. For love of him God imported one hundred pure horses from the sea coast and he pastured them near Mecca.'

The more horses a tribe has, the more feared it is by its neighbours and the greater its defeated neighbours unite for revenge, and soon both the riders and the horses are annihilated. Hence the saying: 'The horse reins are snakes, and death dwells on their backs.'

The Prophet is said to have likened the Arab horse to an arrow in battle and wanted every Muslim warrior to possess one. 'The horse', he said, 'brings fortune in defeat.' Umar quoted him later as also saying of the horse, 'He who loves his mare and treats her kindly shall have God's bounty, but he who ill-treats his mare shall be cursed of

God. After woman came the horse, for the enjoyment and happiness of man.'

Muhammad owned 15 mares over his lifetime. Bought in the markets of the Najd, they were used to breed horses for his army – at the battle of Badr the Muslims had only two horses. He is also said to have established racing to improve both horses and riders. The first of his horses was bought from a Bedouin of the Bani Fasara tribe. Her name was *al-sakbah*, 'the outpouring'. In the early battles of Islam, this mare was always among the horses in the first charge. *Al-sakbah* was a black mare with a white star on her forehead, and her off-fore was touched with white. The Bedouin seldom used saddles. Muhammad was once thrown off his mare and fell against a palm tree, spraining his foot. Thereafter he preferred to ride a camel, mule or donkey.

In this chapter we have caught glimpses of two Bedouin sheikhs: Ibn Jenayb of the Rwalla and Auda abu Tayi of the Bani Howeitat. During my time as a soldier with the Arab Legion I was fortunate to meet and get to know a third, Mithgal al-Faiz, who had become paramount chief of the Bani Sakhr in 1922.

*A Bedu sheikh has no paid retainers on whom he can rely to carry out his orders. He is merely the first among equals in a society where every man is intensely independent and quick to resent any hint of autocracy. His authority depends in consequence on the force of his own personality and his skill in handling men.*

WILFRED THESIGER, *ARABIAN SANDS* (1959)

By now you will have begun to form an idea in your mind of what a Bedouin tribe expected of its leader or sheikh. His role was simply to be the leader. He was responsible for decisions, but he made them only after consultation. He held the tribe together like the shepherd of a flock. He cared for individuals – do you remember how Ibn Jeneyb had cared for his dying tribesman in his own tent and met his dying wish?

Leadership within the tribe was both elective and hereditary. Each tribe or sub-tribe would have a ruling kin, brothers and cousins from whom the chief would normally be chosen. While there was no formal election, tribesmen would offer their loyalties to the member of the ruling kin who most impressed them as a potential leader.

Apart from the qualities of *muruwwa* – courage, generosity, integrity, fairness, and honour or good reputation – a Bedouin chief needed practical wisdom, for he needed to be a skilled negotiator, to be able to resolve quarrels between his followers before they got out of hand, and to deal with allies from other tribes.

Chiefs also had to have intelligence and experience – the sort of judgement that meant that they knew where the fickle desert rain had recently fallen and where they could find the small but succulent patches of grazing that would mean their followers and their flocks could eat and drink well. For the decision to move camp – for better or worse – was always his prerogative. When he gave the signal by striking his tent and packing up his goods on his camels, the whole tribe followed his lead.

A successful chief needed to keep an open tent, for the famed hospitality of the Bedouin can be seen as a part of a complex survival strategy: guests would certainly be welcomed, fed and entertained, but in exchange they would be expected to share their news about grazing conditions, tribal movements and disputes, and all else that counted as news in the desert. All leaders need to keep themselves well informed.

Although tribal chiefs were expected to lead their fellow tribesmen in battle, age and infirmity eventually meant that they delegated that role to a younger warrior. The tribal chief might concentrate on reconciling disputes and on making external alliances, where his wisdom could come best into play. Meanwhile the *qa'id* busied himself with the engrossing task of mounting camel-raids on enemy tribes, or chasing after and tracking down raiders who had ridden off with the tribe's camels and horses. As the Bedouins were accustomed to say: *We take and are ourselves taken.*

The Bedouin chief was expected to personify the Arab virtue of generosity, especially to a guest. And if he was known for his open-handedness it brought him a good reputation. Meals provided, then, for the poor and needy, for the stranger and wayfarer, bring prestige. Generosity and hospitality were considered the cardinal Arabian virtues, and to be thought niggardly would be the ruin of a man. *Every guest brings a blessing*, the noblest of all Arab proverbs says: hence the greeting of the pre-Islamic desert Arabs, *Ahlan wa-sahlan*, 'You have come to a folk who will shelter you and a safe place at which to alight.'

As one Arab poet wrote, 'When you have prepared the meal, entreat to partake thereof a guest – I am not one to eat, like a churl, alone – some traveller through the night, or protégé, for in truth I fear the reproachful talk of men after I am gone.'

No Bedouin wished to be outdone in showing kindness to a guest in his tent – or to be shamed by the charge of not being open-handed or magnanimous. Here all men were equal, for poverty was no cause of reproof among the desert nomads. A poor Bedouin who killed and cooked his last lamb or kid for a guest would receive more honour among his tribe than a great chief whose roasted young camel came from such a large herd that it would be scarcely missed. All tribal societies tend to gauge true generosity on these relativities with remarkable accuracy. Even if a Bedouin robe was worn and patched, his tent sparsely furnished, his wealth limited to a few sheep and goats and his children hungry, he could still be noble in his hospitality. As the proverb says, *The pure-bred mare is not shamed by its trappings.*

This Bedouin virtue of generosity continued to be held in great honour down the ages. Five years after my own military experience with the Bedouin soldiers of the Arab Legion, the English traveller Wilfred Thesiger published the story of his crossings of the Empty Quarter in Saudi Arabia in a book called *Arabian Sands* (1959). We share in Thesiger's effort to judge the virtue of those he met. This makes his encounters into parables:

*Two days later an old man came into our camp. He was limping and even by Bedu standards he looked poor. He wore a torn loin-cloth, thin and grey with age, and carried an ancient rifle... In his belt were two full and six empty cartridge cases, and a dagger with a broken sheath. The Rashid pressed forward to greet him: 'Welcome Bakhit. Long life to you, uncle. Welcome – welcome a hundred times.' I wondered at the warmth of their greetings... I thought, 'He looks a proper old beggar. I bet he asks for something.' Later in the evening he did and I gave him five riyals but by then I had changed my opinion.*

*Bin Kabina said to me: 'Once he was one of the richest men in the tribe, now he has nothing except a few goats.' I asked, 'What happened to his camels? Did raiders take them or did they die of disease?' and Bin Kabina answered, 'No. His generosity ruined him. No one ever came to his tents but he killed a camel to feed them. By God he is generous!' I could hear the envy in his voice.*

Bedouin had a natural, good-mannered respect for tribal elders and they honoured their chiefs. They were never overfamiliar or insolent, but they had no sense of hierarchy: hence the practice of addressing all people by their first name regardless of rank or position, and speaking to them in a direct, open way as if addressing a neighbour while sitting around the hearth where the coffee pots sat upon the glowing stones. The Bedouin soldiers that I knew – men from the Shammar and Rwalla, the Bani Sakhr and Bani Howeitat – all had that peculiar mixture of affectionate regard and simple familiarity that is, as I have said, the special charm of nomadic society.

*They are the most singular and wonderfully clever people I ever saw, but require a great deal of management for they are more desperate and more deep than you can possibly have any idea of… for eloquence and beauty of ideas they are undoubtedly beyond any other people in the world.*

LADY HESTER STANHOPE (1786–1839, ENGLISH TRAVELLER WHO LIVED
WITH THE BEDOUIN NEAR PALMYRA IN 1810)

## KEY POINTS

- *All humankind has passed – or is passing – through a period when the dominant institution of society is the tribe.* This fact has given us innate preferences for certain characteristics in our leaders. We expect them, if they are to fulfil the generic role of *leader*, to be both competent and benevolent.

- *In the harsh conditions of Arabia it was necessary for leaders and followers to live and work together side by side.* Therefore leadership was never hierarchical. A leader was among the people, not over them.

- *Ancestral leaders acquired their office and authority only with the approval of the people.* If not elected by a show of hands or a secret ballot – as is the custom in modern democracies – they were still chosen from a number of eligible candidates.

- *Tribes needed to have one chief who was known to be the man in charge, the one with the chief authority.* The principle of 'unity of command' is universal. An Arab proverb expresses it starkly thus: *The ship that has two captains will sink.*

- *No tribe ever knowingly chooses a man who is known to be morally bad to be its leader.*

- *To ancient peoples, then, it was unthinkable that there should be no leaders. To be without leaders, to obey no one, is unworthy of man: it is to be like the animals*, declares an old proverbial saying from Vietnam. Muhammad was insistent that there should always be a recognized leader, though oddly enough he failed to appoint a successor. Perhaps he trusted his companions to make the right choice.

*O guest of ours, though you have come, though you have honoured us, though you have honoured our dwelling, we in truth are the real guests and you are lord of this tent!*

KING ABDUL AZIZ AL-SAUD OF SAUDI ARABIA'S GREETING

# MUHAMMAD
## 'the Trustworthy One'

*Trust being lost, all the social intercourse of men is brought to naught.*

LIVY (ROMAN HISTORIAN)

During his hidden years in Mecca working with merchant-caravans, probably as a caravan leader, Muhammad acquired a new name: *al-Amin*, the Trustworthy One. The same root, incidentally, gives the English word *amen*, often used at the end of prayers, an expression of hearty approval. We can only guess what it was about the character or conduct of Muhammad that gave rise to this attractive sobriquet, but there is a clue. In 622, while making ready for his migration from Mecca, Muhammad – in danger of his life – delayed long enough to dispose of some moneys that had been deposited at his house.

For centuries the whole life of Mecca centred on its caravan trade. Everyone in Mecca, rich and poor alike, including women landholders (of whom there were a number), was anxious to have a stake in this lucrative business. The powerful families grew richer and more influential with each annual expedition; and the poorer families saved every available dinar in order to share in these commercial ventures. The merchants of Mecca formed themselves into a syndicate, pooling their capital to equip the caravan, and then shared proportionately in the returns from their joint enterprise. Usually a single person would be asked to constitute himself the banker for the occasion, receiving deposits from everyone interested in a particular expedition, and then administer the funds as economically as possible. Most probably it was Muhammad's consistency and scrupulous honesty in this role that earned him his reputation for trustworthiness.

A young widow in Mecca by the name of Khadija bint Khuwaylid more than once entrusted her investment money interest in a caravan into the keeping of one of her cousins – Muhammad. She was so impressed by him professionally, and attracted to him personally, that following a custom allowed among the Arabs – the sexes were much more equal than in other societies – she sent him a proposal of marriage which included the words: 'O son of my uncle [Arabic has no word for cousin],' she wrote in her letter, 'I like you because of our relationship and your high reputation among your people, your trustworthiness and good character and truthfulness.'

Muhammad accepted her proposal. It was one of the wisest decisions he made. His only wife until her death (c618), she bore him Fatima and sons (none survived) and other daughters. And she was the first person to believe in Muhammad's prophethood.

*No man is a prophet in his own land,* said a proverb already ancient in Muhammad's day. He would know the truth of it, for he had to endure years of rejection and even hostility from most of his fellow townsfolk. Through all these trials and tribulations in Mecca, Khadija was Muhammad's chief stay and support. She knew her man and believed him as only a woman in love can. Perhaps these words of the French historian and political scientist Alexis de Tocqueville about his wife may well express what Muhammad felt about his wife: 'She softens, calms and strengthens me in difficulties which disturb me but leave her serene.'

Clearly, then, Muhammad was a man with a reputation for integrity. That word, from the Latin *integer* whole, is especially appropriate for Muhammad as far as Muslims are concerned, for in its primary meaning integrity implies unity that indicates interdependence of the parts and *completeness and perfection of the whole*. Human beings are like stones, some Muslims say, and Muhammad is as the only ruby among them.

Honesty means a refusal to lie, steal or cheat in any way. Integrity goes a mile beyond honesty: it implies *trustworthiness and incorruptibility to a degree that one is incapable of being false to a trust, responsibility or pledge*. A leader with integrity is like the English poet William Wordsworth's 'Happy Warrior':

*Who comprehends his trust, and to the same*
*Keeps faithful, with singleness of aim;*
*And therefore does not stop, nor lie in wait*
*For wealth or honour, or for worldly state.*

This integrity extends through the entireness or wholeness of the character. It is found in small matters as well as great, for allegiance to truth is tested as much by small things as by those that are more important.

Notice the centrality of the value of *truth*, as evidenced by a firm adherence to truth in all things – in the concept of integrity. Khadija, you recall, mentioned Muhammad's 'truthfulness' – that he habitually spoke the truth – as well as his 'trustworthiness', but in fact these two virtues go hand in hand. If you tell the truth, people will trust you; if you lie and the other person finds out, then trust will be diminished if not lost for ever.

Why does truth or veracity, honesty and high principle, matter in a leader? The reason is simple. Leaders who are true, and always speak the truth, create *trust*. And trust is vital in all human relations, professional or private.

You can see why Muhammad insisted upon integrity in those who were chosen to be leaders in the Umma, the growing Muslim community. There was to be no place for any form of bribery or corruption: not that this prohibition was – or is – easy, for man is 'violent... in his love of wealth' (Q100:8).

*I will stand surety for Paradise if you save yourself from six things: telling untruths, violating promises, dishonouring trust, being unchaste in thought and act, striking the first blow, taking what is bad and unlawful.*

MUHAMMAD

Perhaps of all Muhammad's successors it was the second caliph, Umar, who is the chief exemplar of integrity in Islam. Although he lacked Muhammad's humour and charm, Umar matched him in scrupulous honesty and uprightness in matters financial, his passion for impartial justice and his adherence to the simple, open and approachable Bedouin style of leadership. Numani, the authoritative biographer of Umar, emphasizes his unbending integrity:

*Here, we must note that all the Caliph's efforts in this regard would have counted for little if he had not himself led by example. He stressed repeatedly that, as regards the Law, he stood on an equal footing with any other individual. He claimed no special privileges or exemptions as caliph. He proclaimed, instead, that his powers were limited and his exercise of them subject to scrutiny and criticism.*

*Regarding public funds, Umar said: 'I have no greater right on your money [ie public funds] than the guardian of an orphan has on that orphan's property. If I am wealthy, I shall not take anything. If I am needy, I shall take for my maintenance according to usage. You people – you have many rights on me which you should demand of me. One of those rights is that I should not collect revenues and spoils of war unlawfully; the second is that the revenues and spoils of war that come into my possession should not be spent unlawfully; another is that I should increase your salaries and protect the frontiers, and that I should not cast you into unnecessary perils.'*

This is a further reflection especially for Muslim readers. The simple message of Muhammad was in Arabic *tawhid*, the oneness of God:

*Say: He is Allah, the One and Only;*
*Allah, the Eternal, Absolute;*
*He does not beget, nor is He begotten;*
*And there is none like Him.*

Q112

For believers, God has self-evidently many qualities or attributes, or 'names' as they are called in the Islamic tradition. Encouraged by the Qur'an (Q7:180; Q17:110; Q20:8), Muslims selected 99 of these attributes of God describing this perfection, from the Qur'an and traditions. Referred to as 'the most beautiful names of God', they describe a range of characteristics that balance the power of God (the Creator, the Sovereign and the All-Knowing) with His love and mercy (the All-Loving, the Most Gracious and the All-Forgiving). The names are frequently memorized and used in prayers. One name that has been hidden by God is *Ism Allah al-a'zam*, 'The Greatest Name of Allah'. Yet all this unfathomably rich diversity is encompassed in an essential unity: 'Say: He is Allah, the One...'

Integrity, you could say, within this tradition is the counterpart of *tawhid* in a person's life and character. If 'man is made in the likeness of God', then personal integrity reflects the oneness of God.

## KEY POINTS

- *The finest pearls in the world come from the Arabian Gulf.* Pearls were traditionally graded into five kinds. The pearl of highest quality, the perfect pearl, is called *al-Jiwan*. Among all the qualities of leadership, great and small, integrity is *al-Jiwan*.

- *Integrity implies such rectitude that one is incorruptible or incapable of being false to a trust or a responsibility or to one's own standards.* As the Latin proverb says: *Integrity is the noblest possession.*

- *There can be no confidence without truth.* If you want to lose the confidence of your team, try any of the following behaviours: dishonesty, duplicity, deceitfulness, lying, dissimulation or manipulation.

- *'Trust, like the soul, once gone is gone for ever' (Catullus, Roman poet, c84–54 BCE).*

- *Those occupying leadership roles who completely lack integrity are what we call 'blind shepherds'.* They are not really 'bad' leaders, because they are not leaders at all: they are *misleaders*. Woe to the people afflicted with them! As an ancient Hebrew proverb says: *When God wants to punish the sheep he sends them a blind shepherd.*

*People think of leaders as men or women devoted to service, and by service they mean that they serve their followers... The real leader serves truth, not people.*

N B YEATS, *LETTERS TO HIS SON W B YEATS* (1944)

# 6

# Sharing in
# HARDSHIP

*When his work is done, his aim fulfilled,*
*They will all say, 'We did this ourselves.'*

LAO-TZU, 6TH CENTURY BCE

It is a fundamental and universal principle of leadership that good leaders take their full share in the dangers and hardship of their people. By hardship I mean that which is hard to bear: privation, suffering, toil, fatigue, oppression, injury, injustice and the like. Great leaders who accept their destiny and take this 'steep and thorny path' to leadership – such as Mahatma Gandhi in India or Nelson Mandela in Africa – acquire something that is rarely conferred upon a leader – *moral authority*.

When the small community of believers in the One God were harassed and even persecuted in Mecca by the majority of the Quraysh, who were trying to prevent the disruption of their traditional way of life, Muhammad had shared in their hardship. Together they went into a self-imposed exile from their beloved but dangerous home town. In Medina, their destination, they found themselves in a large oasis that spread out its green fingers into the surrounding desert. It was well populated, however, with the villages of various tribal groups.

It was soon after the arrival of the Muslims in Medina, when they set to work to build what was in effect the world's first mosque, that the Prophet Muhammad laboured with the Arab builders and craftsmen as if he was one of them. And as they worked, inspired by Muhammad's presence and example, the men began to sing – always a sign of high spirits. The song, doubtless made up as they went along, was a humorous one:

*If we sat down while the Prophet worked,*
*It could be said that we had shirked.*

None of them wanted the reputation of being the man who took it easy while the Prophet toiled in the sun. Such is the power of example.

The Qurayshi Muslims from Mecca, known in Arabic as the *Muhajirun* (Emigrants), and the Muslims from the two semi-nomadic tribes of Medina – the *Ansar* (Helpers) – were now working as one team with a common task, for they shared a common faith in God and in a heaven beyond death that they would surely enter:

*There's no life but the life of the next world*
*O God, have mercy on the Muhajirun and the Ansar.*

A former slave in Medina, now one of the Muhajirun, caused some merriment when, full of complaints, he staggered back to the building site bent almost double with a basket packed with dried mud-bricks on his back. He even saw fit – to much laughter – to complain loudly to Muhammad: 'These people are killing me!' he kept repeating. 'They load me up with burdens that they can't carry themselves!' Muhammad's reply is unfortunately not recorded.

*When people are of one mind and heart, they can move Mount Tai. [Tai was a famous mountain in Shangdou Province, the highest known to Confucius.]*

CONFUCIUS

'I am a worker', Muhammad once said. If there was work to do – such as digging the defensive ditch around parts of Medina in 627 CE – he took up a spade or pickaxe and dug with the rest of them. He carried baskets of earth on his shoulders, and joined in their song. Salman al-Farsi recalled working with a pickaxe in a ditch when a large rock obstructed him and he struggled to break it. The Prophet saw his efforts and came over to help him. He took the pickaxe from his hand and gave such a blow that the rock was split in two.

Muhammad seems to have been more than ready to share in any work in progress, even domestic chores. Anas ibn Malik, who worked as a servant to the Prophet in his later years, recalled: 'He served me more than I served him! He has never been angry with me. He never treated me harshly.'

Muhammad just could not sit back and watch while others worked. While journeying through the desert one day he and his small company made camp in the early evening. One of his companions offered to buy a sheep from a Bedouin encampment nearby. Others volunteered to kill, skin and cook it. Muhammad was already on his feet gathering thorn bushes for the fire. They pressed him to rest. He replied that he knew they could do everything without his help, but that he did not wish to be idle while his friends were busy.

When I read the above story I am reminded of the young Muhammad, who, if my speculation is correct, once rode his camel as a caravan leader. He enjoyed such conversations on the journey, and the story is a good illustration of his saying: 'On a journey the leader of a people is their servant.'

Muhammad's willingness to listen and to take advice from others also helped him and the Muslim commanders to make wise strategic decisions. As the story of Auda abu Tayi's raid shows (see Chapter 4), the control of water wells was literally a matter of life or death in a desert battle.

Just before the battle of Badr in 624 CE, Muhammad accompanied an advance guard sent out to secure the nearest well to Badr from the direction of Medina. Once there they halted to rest. But a Bedouin called Hubab al-Jamuh of the Bani Salama who was in the party and who knew the area well approached the Prophet.

'Is this a place which God has ordered you to occupy,' he asked, 'so that we can neither advance nor withdraw from it, or is it a matter of opinion and military tactics?'

Muhammad replied that it was the latter. Then Hubab pointed out to him that it was not the right place to stop. They should press on to the well nearest to the enemy, halt there and stop up the wells behind it. For themselves they should construct a cistern so that they would have plenty of water. Then they could fight their enemy, who would have nothing to drink. The Prophet said that this was an excellent plan and agreed to it. They acted upon it immediately: the wells were stopped, and a cistern was built and filled with water from which his men replenished their drinking vessels.

The immediate preliminaries of Badr, when about 300 Muslims faced over 1,000 Meccans, give us another vivid glimpse of Muhammad in action as a leader. Notice his calmness and confidence, based upon a complete trust in Allah. Leaders who smile and joke in the face of such odds release the tension in their soldiers; they radiate confidence.

Muhammad, as always, was sharing in the work that needed doing – in this case drawing up the Muslims in their formations.

*Truly Allah loves those who fight in solid lines for His Cause, like a well-compacted wall.*

Q61:4

As Muhammad was walking up the line straightening it with an arrow in his hand, he came to one Sawadi ibn Ghaziya, who was standing too far out of line.

'Stand in line, O Sawadi!' the Prophet said, gently pricking him in the belly with his arrow.

'You have hurt me, O Apostle of God', Sawadi cried, with a much exaggerated cry of pain. 'God has sent you to teach us about right and justice, so please allow me to retaliate.'

'Take your retaliation', said Muhammad with a smile, uncovering his own belly. Sawadi kissed it and embraced him.

'O Messenger of God,' he said, 'you see what is before us, and I may not survive the battle, and as this is my last time with you I want my skin to touch yours.'

Muhammad then blessed him. With soldiers like that you tend not to lose battles.

Muhammad could be severe enough when the situation required it. Such a situation arose after the disastrous

Muslim defeat at the battle of Uhud, just outside Medina. In battle he wore a helmet and one or sometimes two coats of chain-mail made of the finest-quality steel.

*He made you garments to protect you from heat, and coats of mail to protect you in your wars.*

Q16:81

A bodyguard mounted on horses always accompanied him. Even so Muhammad narrowly escaped death at Uhud. A stone from a sling split his upper lip and broke one of his front teeth; another blow from a rock drove two rings of the chain-mail under his helmet into his flesh and blood poured from the gash in his forehead. He fell to the ground stunned, but was carried away to safety.

You can imagine that Muhammad was not best pleased when he heard afterwards that during the battle one of the Muslim soldiers – a member of the tribe called the Bani al-Aws – had used the opportunity of the battlefield confusion when the Muslims were routed to kill the object of a tribal blood-feud, a Bani al-Khazraj tribesman fighting alongside him. Someone saw the deed and reported it. A careful investigation confirmed what had happened.

The offence was more than a flagrant breach of military discipline on the battlefield. By putting his tribal need for revenge – and his own personal honour – above the interests of the team as a whole he had contributed to the collapse of the Muslim order on that day. Moreover, by killing a companion-in-arms in this way he had offended Bedouin law. The power of the small Muslim army had also been reduced by one precious man. Lastly, his action could be construed as an offence against God and the sacred cause. Something had to be done, as otherwise Muslim soldiers would lose their respect for the leaders.

Never a man to delegate to others an unpleasant job, Muhammad had his donkey brought to him and he rode along to the mosque of the offender's tribe in one of the villages scattered among the groves of palm trees in the oasis of Medina. Finding the chiefs of the al-Aws assembled there, Muhammad conferred with them and then directed them to bring the offender into the open and execute him immediately. As Muhammad mounted his donkey the culprit rushed forward, grasped his feet and begged for mercy, but the Prophet turned his face away. Such was the need to build teamwork so that each Muslim soldier trusted his neighbour in the ranks as if he was his brother.

After the battle of Hunain against the Bani Hawazin, you may recall (see Chapter 1), Muhammad had at last managed with considerable political acumen to settle the issue concerning the Hawazin women and children. Immediately he was faced with another problem. As the Prophet moved away to complete the arrangement for the return of the families to their menfolk, a crowd of Bedouins from the different tribes who had fought in the battle now followed him like a swarm of flies.

'O Messenger, divide the spoil of camels and sheep among us', they kept soliciting him insistently and urgently in their loud Bedouin voices. They tugged at his cloak so hard that it was pulled off his shoulders and trampled underfoot in the pressing throng. Eventually Muhammad put his back against an acacia tree and faced his importunate tormentors.

'Give me back my cloak', he pleaded good-humouredly. 'By God, if I had as many sheep as the trees on the plain by the sea I would give them all to you!'

When the camels were eventually divided, Muhammad made from his own share some characteristically generous gifts: a hundred camels each to four prominent Meccans of his own tribe the Quraysh, until recently his bitterest enemies, and similar presents to two chiefs from the desert nomad tribes who had embraced Islam and fought hard at Hunayn.

It was now the turn of the Muslims of Medina – the 'Helpers' – to feel that they had not been treated with justice. Had they not been the first to rally to Muhammad after that first panic-stricken retreat? As they had done the lion's share of the fighting, should they not be feeding first at the carcass? Yet inexplicably they had received no camels.

Sa'ad ibn Ubada, the chief of one of the two tribes of the 'Helpers' concerned, told Muhammad what they were saying behind his back.

'How do you yourself feel on the question, Sa'ad?' asked Muhammad.

'I feel with my people', replied the chief simply.

'Then collect them together and I will speak with them', answered the Prophet.

'O Helpers,' he began, 'what is this that I hear of you? Do you think ill of me in your hearts? Did I not come to you when you were erring and God guided you; poor and God made you rich; enemies and God softened your hearts? Why don't you answer me? Does generosity only belong to God and his Messenger?' The Prophet paused, and then continued: 'Had you so wished you could have said "You came to us discredited, and we believed in you; deserted and we helped you; a fugitive and we took you in; poor and we comforted you." In saying this, you would have spoken the truth', Muhammad told them. 'Are you disturbed in your minds because of the good things of this life by which I win over a people that they may become Muslims, while I entrust you to your reliance upon God?' he asked them. 'Are you not satisfied that other men should take away flocks and herds, while you take the Messenger of God back with you to Medina? If all men went one way and the Helpers the other, I should take the way of the Helpers. May God have mercy on the Helpers, their sons and their sons' sons.'

Such was the effect of Muhammad's words that the men of Medina burst into tears and – as the Bedouin say – they wept until their beards were wet. That is leadership.

In the spring of 622 Muhammad decided on a peaceful march to Mecca to perform the three-day pilgrimage. With a thousand devout followers, carrying swords but no bows or lances, he set out on the march south. But the Quraysh were determined to deny them access to the Kaaba.

After protracted negotiations at the Muslim camp in the valley of Hudaibiya, eight miles from Mecca, Muhammad seemed to accept defeat. He concluded a 10-year truce with the Quraysh that was less than popular with many of his followers. Umar in particular was incensed.

'Are you not God's Prophet?' he demanded. 'Are we not in the right and our enemies in the wrong? Then why yield in such a base way against the honour of our religion?' He was merely echoing the questions being asked through the tents of the Muslims.

When the Quraysh envoys had departed, the Prophet decided anyway to sacrifice the 70 garlanded camels they had brought with them for the expected rites at the Kaaba. He went out to address his followers.

'Rise and sacrifice your animals and shave your heads', he directed them. In other words they were to pretend that their campsite at Hudaybiya was the sacred place inside Mecca.

The Muslim pilgrims, however, remained seated; not a man stirred.

'Rise and sacrifice your animals and shave your heads', he commanded them. Again, not a man moved.

After a third command had failed, Muhammad turned and in sorrow entered his tent. Never had his authority been so challenged in public. One of his wives, Umm Salama, had travelled with him and now she awaited him in his tent. She advised Muhammad to go out immediately, walk in silence past the seated Muslims and perform the very actions he had commanded.

Muhammad listened to her advice. He descended into the valley and approached his own camel, garlanded in readiness for the sacrifice. He prepared the noble beast for the knife with the blessing 'In the Name of God, God is most great' (*Bism-Allah, Allahu Akbar*). The power of leading from the front worked. The Muslims hastened to follow his example, and the crisis of confidence was over.

*Remember that your position does not give you the right to command. It only lays upon you the duty of so living your life that others may receive your orders without being humiliated.*

DAG HAMMARSKJÖLD, FORMER SECRETARY-GENERAL

OF THE UNITED NATIONS

# KEY POINTS

- *By sharing in the labours, dangers and hardships of his people Muhammad exemplified a universal principle of good leadership.* It is what – deep down – people expect of their leaders, and when it doesn't happen it always produces adverse comment.

- *There is the authority of* position *and the authority of* knowledge – *'Authority flows from the one who knows.'* But sharing in hardship confers upon a leader something quite rare – *moral authority.*

- *Such conduct by the best leaders wins them more than the respect of their people – it attracts their love.* And love is the greatest power in the world. As Huananzi wrote in a classic Taoist text:

*In ancient times good generals always were in the vanguard themselves. They didn't set up canopies in the heat and didn't wear leather in the cold; thus they experienced the same heat and cold as their soldiers.*

*They did not ride over rough terrain, always dismounting when climbing hills; thus they experienced the same toil as their soldiers.*

*They would eat only after food had been cooked for the troops, and they would drink only after water had been drawn for the troops; thus they experienced the same hunger and thirst as their soldiers.*

*In battle they would stand within range of enemy fire; thus they experienced the same dangers as their soldiers.*

*So in their military operations, good generals always use accumulated gratitude to attack accumulated bitterness, and accumulated love to attack accumulated hatred. Why would they not win?*

*A leader is best*
*When people barely know that he exists.*
*Not so good when people obey and acclaim him,*
*Worst when they despise him.*
*Fail to honour people,*
*They fail to honour you.*
*But of a good leader, who talks little,*
*When his work is done, his aim fulfilled,*
*They will all say, 'We did this ourselves.'*

LAO-TZU, 6TH CENTURY BCE

# 7

# HUMILITY

*Humility and courtesy are themselves ways of reverencing God.*

MUHAMMAD

Muhammad's vocation was to be a *rasul*, meaning messenger (of God). It is one of two Quranic terms to refer to Muhammad and other prophets. The other is *nabi*, usually translated as 'prophet'. The Qur'an appears to use the two terms interchangeably.

The role of *rasul*, however, implies the more emissary function of delivering a message in specified or given language. The prophet, from the Greek *prophetes*, interpreter, spokesman (of the will of God), communicates a divinely inspired message in the form of spiritual insights and moral teachings. It also has to be *truth through personality*, for if the message is not exemplified in the prophet's life he can be discounted as a hypocrite.

In the Hebrew scriptures the distinctive outward sign of a *nabi* was his loose outward garment. Muhammad certainly had a mantle or cloak: he sometimes wrapped himself in it, and, falling into a trance, he received his inspirations. Think of that cloak, for a moment, as being a metaphor for role. When Muhammad put on the cloak he was – so to speak – speaking and acting in his appointed role.

In his prophetic role Muhammad seems to have been far from humble: he would brook no opposition, tolerate no rivals and accept no compromises. You were either for him or against him: it was a simple black-or-white choice. And he insisted that his name as God's Messenger and Prophet should stand highest among all prophets not just in his lifetime but for all time. Moreover, Muhammad seems to have claimed the right – and exercised it – of directly or indirectly causing the execution of at least some of those whom he judged to be 'enemies of God' in actively opposing his message. In other words, although so often merciful – even to his worst enemies – on occasions he could be utterly ruthless.

To a non-Muslim that may well sound like a monumental form of arrogance (Latin *arrogare*, to claim for oneself) on the part of Muhammad. How can any man claim to know the will of God in this way? Or to have uttered the last word about God as far as humankind is concerned? But, of course, that is not how Muhammad or his devout followers saw the situation. God has spoken, and that was the end of the matter.

It is clear, then, that – in his role as Prophet – Muhammad was not a reasonable man, not even by the standards of his day. But reasonable men do not change the world.

Incidentally, changing his world was not easy. *Change throws up the need for leaders, and leaders bring about change*. But Arabia, still basically a desert nomad society, was unchanging, deeply traditional, deeply set in its *sunna*, way of life or custom. Any man who challenged its beliefs and values would do so on peril of his life. Where there is no change it is impossible to lead.

Muhammad's approach – if I can call it that – was the only one possible in such a society. He had been called and sent, he said, to *remove* changes, to restore Mecca to its original state as the centre of Abraham's religion of the One God. In the Qur'an, Abraham is mentioned 69 times. In fact only Moses – perhaps the forerunner that Muhammad most admired – received more references (136). Abraham is described as a prophet (Q19:42; cf Genesis 20:7), with a religion named after him (*din Ibrahim*, Q16:124, Q22:77), with his own scripture (*suhuf Ibrahim*, Q53:35, Q87:18). In conjunction with his son Ishmael, above all, Abraham establishes the first temple to *El* at Mecca.

Like some of his Meccan contemporaries, Muhammad – a follower of the religion of Abraham – may well have become a *hanif* before his calling to be the Messenger of Allah to the Arabs, for the tradition that Abraham had given the torch of his faith in the One God to Ishmael, and through him to his descendants the Arabs, was known in Arabia well before Muhammad was born. A Greek source, *The Ecclesiastical History of Sozomen*, written in the 5th century CE, tells us as much. Sozomen was a native of Gaza and his mother tongue was Arabic, so we have testimony from a reliable source that by the 5th century some Arabs, at least in that area, were familiar with the idea that they were Abrahamic monotheists by origin; how far this was true of Arabs in other parts of the peninsula it is impossible to say.

The ancestral tribe – mother and father of all the Semites – who inhabited central Arabia long before the days of

Abraham had a name for the Creator – God or High God over all gods – *El*. Allah, the name of God among Muslims, is normally the same word (Arabic: *al* the + *ilah* god). It is found in different forms in other Semitic cultures. Israel – originally a nickname given to Jacob – means 'he who wrestles with *El*'. Jesus died with the Aramaic cry 'Eli, Eli... my God, my God...' on his parched lips.

Building on the legend that the Ka'ba in Mecca was once a centre for the worship of *El*, Muhammad gave the Arabs a new story of their past, one that greatly exalted their dignity and significance in history. In essence it was that Abraham had come in person to Mecca and there, in obedience to God, offered as the commanded sacrifice not Sarah's son Isaac but Hagar's son Ishmael. In other words, the Arabs too who stood in direct line of spiritual descent – the true monotheists (Arabic: *hanif*). The genealogy of Abraham's descent had, as it were, been corrected by a direct divine revelation.

*You are the best peoples, evolved for mankind, enjoining what is right, forbidding what is wrong, and believing in Allah.*

*Thus have We made you an umma [community] justly balanced, that you might be witnesses over the nations...*

Q2:143

Ibn Ishaq tells us a well-authenticated story about Muhammad. It concerns a conversation between Abu Amir – a resident of Medina – and the Prophet. Abu Amir somewhat boldly asked Muhammad what religion he had brought to Medina.

'The Hanifiyya, the religion of Abraham', replied the Prophet.

'That is what I follow', said Abu Amir.

'You do not', came the retort.

'But I do!' insisted Abu Amir. He continued: 'You, Muhammad, have introduced into the Hanifiyya things which do not belong to it.'

'I have not', said the Prophet. 'I have brought it pure and white.'

'May God let the liar die a lonely, homeless fugitive!' said Abu Amir, doubtless with Muhammad in mind.

'Well and good. May God so reward him!' said Muhammad.

Ibn Ishaq took some pleasure in declaring that events proved Abu Amir – 'the enemy of God' – was the liar. He left Medina to go to Mecca, and when Muhammad conquered it he went to Taif; when Taif became Muslim he went to Syria and died there in self-imposed exile.

Without entering into the theological or philosophical issues at stake in the truth-claims of Muhammad, from the leadership angle I can see the logic in Muhammad's deter-mined takeover and monopolizing of the role of prophet. One God, One Prophet – the banner of Islam – is at its sublime level simply an application of the principle of unity of command. *Where shepherds are lost, sheep are lost*, says a Bulgarian proverb.

If Muhammad *had* allowed other prophets in the Arabian peninsula – they did arise, men both influential in their tribes and eager to work alongside Muhammad – his architectural vision of the new theology and the new community could have become fragmented in his lifetime. A Russian proverb captures humankind's experience in a nutshell: *Seven shepherds, no flock.*

Once Muhammad, however, had so to speak put aside his prophet's cloak – the role of Messenger – he was the same man, he who had led merchant-caravans and slept in Khadija's arms. For the clear-cut division between God and man is central to *tawhid*. Muhammad's constant emphasis *that he was only a man* – no more, no less – is part of the message he was commissioned to deliver.

It follows that the humility that Muhammad exemplified was not a special grace granted to a prophet who had seen the vision of God or talked with God as if with a friend. It was said of Moses, for example, that he was 'very meek, more than all men that were on the face of the earth' (Numbers 12:3). It was the humility that is proper to all persons in relation to God, and especially to the Arabs, a proud but poor people who by humbling themselves before God in Islam (Arabic: *islam*, from *aslama*, to submit, to surrender) had been raised to a sudden greatness among the nations.

During his caliphate, Umar ibn al-Khattab was marching upon Damascus with his army. Abu Ubayda was with him. They came upon a little lake. Umar descended from his camel, took off his shoes, tied them together and hung them on his shoulder. He then took the halter off his camel and they entered the water together. Seeing this in front of the army, Abu Ubayda could not contain himself.

'O Commander of the Believers,' he said, 'how can you be so humble in front of all your men?'

'Woe to you, Abu Ubayda!' replied Umar. 'If only no one else other than you thought this way! Thoughts like this will cause the downfall of the Muslims. Don't you see we were indeed a very lowly people? God raised us to a position of honour and greatness through Islam. If we forget who we are and wish other than the Islam which elevated us, the One who raised us surely will debase us.'

Humility derives from the Latin word *humus*, earth. From the same root comes our name – *homo, hominis*, human being. We are made of the earth, as it is said, and to the earth we shall return. The Anglo-Saxon equivalent gives us the word *lowly*. Humility or lowliness means to acknowledge that one is a human being – no more and no less – and not God.

*Do not strut arrogantly about the earth, for you cannot break it open nor can you match the mountains in height.*

Q17:37

Humility in this creaturely sense is a virtue in any person, whether or not they believe in a creator. Those privileged to explore the wonders of the universe as astronomers or physicists, naturalists or space travellers, often report a visitation of humility: an awesome greatness that measures their own stature without diminishing it.

*And turn not your face away from men with pride, nor walk in insolence through the earth. Verily, God likes not each arrogant boaster.*

Q31:18

Such a sense of humility is most valuable in those who occupy high offices of leadership among us. 'Power tends to corrupt, and absolute power to corrupt absolutely', wrote the historian Lord Acton, in a letter to scholar and ecclesiastic Mandell Creighton, dated April 1887. The worst corruption of all for a leader is to believe – and encourage others to believe – that one is more than a person, superhuman, semi-divine, even in the most extreme cases God. Here is the ultimate form of idolatry that Muhammad set his face against.

Humility not only inoculates leaders against what the Greeks called *hubris*, the insolent pride that outrages heaven. It is also an antidote against the lesser but far more common forms of pride: arrogance and overbearingness.

Because of their exaggerated sense of self, *arrogant* people take upon themselves more power or authority than is rightly theirs. By contrast humble people know their limitations: they know what they know, and they know what they do not know; they know what they can do or be, and they know what they cannot do or be. As a consequence, they are not unwilling to heed advice, even when it is unsolicited, or to ask for and accept help.

As you will recall, when Muhammad was not speaking *ex cathedra* (Latin 'from the chair' – with authority) in his role as prophet to the Muslim community, he was ready to listen to advice, and even change his decision in the light of what he had heard. In other words, he could be both consistent as a person and yet infinitely flexible as a leader. Any plan is bad that is not susceptible to change.

The Arabs of Muhammad's day were not like docile sheep; they responded only to effective leadership, but they were difficult to manage or handle. Umar, the second caliph, knew as much, hence his prayer on taking office: 'Almighty God, I am harsh, make me mild; I am weak, give me strength. For the Arab is a sensitive-nosed camel and his rope has been placed in my hand, and surely I will keep him on the path, seeking the help of God.' Umar's prayer exemplified humility. He seeks the strength and guidance of God, acknowledging his own weakness. As the Arab proverb says, *When God wishes a man well, he gives him insight into his faults.* Umar was a tough old Arab commander, a veteran. His fault was harshness in dealing with people. *Harsh* in English, meaning 'rough', comes from an old German word that literally meant 'hairy': there was nothing smooth about Umar. A harsh manager is insensitive, inconsiderate, severe and unpleasant.

But Umar wanted to develop himself as a leader, partly because he knew that the Arabs would not respond well to his manner and partly because he had seen in Muhammad an example of how it should be done. The way of leadership was to be both tough and demanding but fair on the one hand, and on the other hand gentle, warm and kind. When these two 'eyes' were balanced in one 'sight', so that it came naturally, then you could lead the Arabs – or any other people for that matter. But you always demanded more from yourself than you asked of others.

*By an act of mercy from God, you [Prophet] were gentle in your dealings with them – had you been harsh, or hard-hearted, they would have dispersed and left you – so pardon them and ask forgiveness for them. Consult with them about matters, then, when you have decided on a course of action, put your trust in God: God loves those who put their trust in him.*

Q3:159

Here are Muhammad's waymarks on leadership, both for himself and for his unknown successors, and indeed for all who are called to serve others in the role of leadership. To be gentle suggests that you avoid extremes, that you use no more than a slight use of force to gain a result, and that you show a tender consideration for others.

This avoidance of extremes – an essentially moderate approach – was characteristic of Muhammad. The Qur'an reflects his own practical wisdom in religious practice as in living life generally. In fact, wisdom (Arabic: *hikma*) is prominent in the Qur'an in the form of simple moral principles. For example, some Bedouins made themselves beggars by giving away all they had in open-handed hospitality to the passing wayfarer, in order to be famous in desert society. The Quranic wisdom counters both extremes: 'Do not behave as if your hand were tied to your throat [ie don't be miserly]; but do not stretch it out completely [ie be prodigal], for then you will be either reproached or reduced to penury' (Q17:29).

In Medina, Muhammad lived in the long, low, mud-brick house with open windows with a palm-leaf roof that he had helped to build with his own hands. It was more like a Bedouin tent than a town house. It was divided into partitions for his wives, and Muhammad – again like a Bedouin 'lord of the tent' – had no sleeping quarters of his own. There was no sanitation, so nature's needs had to be met by walking out into the desert nearby. Muhammad later introduced a curtain such as the one that divides the Bedouin black tent in the desert, so that his wives would not be stared at by the numerous visitors who came to meet him. He never ate at a table but always kneeling or squatting on the ground in the open air in the Bedouin manner. There was no carpet, simply a woven palm mat. He used only his right hand to eat, seldom a knife. He preferred the simple dress and patched *'aba* or cloak such as that worn by a Bedouin chief who had impoverished himself by his generosity.

When a host sent a servant or child to conduct the Prophet to his house, Muhammad never walked ahead in front of the others like a dignitary with followers. He allowed the servant or child the dignity of leading the way. Often he followed the Bedouin custom of being led by hand to their destination by the messenger who had been sent to fetch him. That custom, incidentally, was still the practice of my Bedouin friends when I was a soldier in the Arab Legion in the middle of the last century.

Muhammad would never allow a seat to be reserved for him when attending a meeting but would sit wherever there was an empty place. When men rose to their feet as he walked by, he would ask them to remain standing only if that was their way of showing respect for humankind. If they were standing up to honour him, however, he always asked them to sit down. For Muhammad said to them: 'I am a man like you. I eat food like you and I also sit down when I am tired – like you!' Sometimes, when tired, he would greet visitors on his knees or while sitting on the ground. In other words, he would accept no special privileges for himself.

*The true servants of the Most Gracious God are those*
*who walk on earth with humility, and when the ignorant*
*address them, they say 'Peace!'*

Q25:63

A story from the early Syrian Christian tradition about Jesus, preserved by Muslim editors, illustrates this saying in the Qur'an:

*The Messiah passed by a company of Jews, who cursed him, but he blessed them. It was said to him: 'They speak you evil and you speak them well!' He answered: 'Everyone spends of that which he has.'*

When Muhammad met people he gave them his full attention, turning towards them as he spoke to them. With warmth he clasped their hands affectionately; it was said he was never the first to withdraw his hand from that of another. In conversation with someone he never looked over the other person's shoulder, as if he wanted to talk to someone more important or interesting. Nor did he ever look bored or distracted. People always remembered his face.

*On another occasion, a man new to the Muslim gathering came to visit the Prophet. The man was filled with awe that made him nervous and anxious; this was natural for the man as his belief told him he was visiting the Prophet of God and the leader of the powerful Muslim nation.*

*When the Prophet realized the man's uneasiness, he comforted him saying, 'Brother, don't be afraid; relax and be at ease. I am not a great monarch or king. I am only a son of a lady who ate cured meat.'*

IBN MAJAH

Muhammad disliked the kind of gossip that speaks ill of people behind their backs. He was always careful to preserve a person's honour or reputation. For example, he never found fault with people in public, though he could be very truthful and firm with individuals in private.

There is no record of Muhammad ever losing his temper or striking a man in anger. He saw displays of uncontrollable fury as a vice in leaders, not a virtue – and a sin against God. 'You ask for a piece of advice', Muhammad once said to a leader. 'I tell you: do not get angry.' He lived by his own words here and expected his fellow Muslims to do so as well: not always successfully, I may add, but Muhammad was also a charitable man. He tended to see the best in people, and to put his cloak over their faults and failings. He abided by the spirit of the Arab proverb: *Deal as gently with the faults of others as you do with your own.*

When displeased with someone Muhammad turned the palms of his hands away from the person or fingered his beard. From evidence in the Qur'an he clearly disliked people leaving meetings without his leave, and people who talked too loudly at him – some Bedouins in particular tend to have loud and rather rasping voices.

Ali ibn Abi Talib (died 661 CE) was the son-in-law of the Prophet Muhammad, and in 656 was chosen to be the fourth caliph. His numerous sermons, letters and other tracts were collected following his death and published under the title *Nahj al-balagha* (Peak of Eloquence). Here he often expresses his views on leadership in letters to his administrators and military commanders. In the Document of Instruction, written for Malik al-Nashtar, the governor of Egypt, Ali declares that leaders are governed by the same laws as ordinary people. They have no special status – not, at least, in the eyes of God. He also makes it plain that the leader has an equal duty to all subjects, regardless of rank: 'The way most coveted by you should be that which is the most equitable for the right, the most universal by way of justice.' Repeatedly, he stresses the need for justice, equity and even-handedness.

But it is the relationship between leaders and followers that takes primacy in Ali's ideas. In a striking passage from the Document of Instruction, he instructs leaders to be always accessible to their people: 'Then, do not keep yourself secluded from the people for a long time, because the seclusion of those in authority from the subjects is a kind of narrow-sightedness and causes ignorance about their affairs.'

In a long and moving letter to his son and successor al-Hasan, written while he was dying, Ali writes about leadership as being a calling or vocation and urges leaders to be humble and not seek riches for their own personal ends. He charges his son to be ever vigilant and prepared for change. 'Often a person with eyes misses the track while a blind person finds the correct path. Whoever takes the world to be safe, it will betray him. Whoever regards the world as great, it will humiliate him. When authority changes, the time changes too.' In other words, a wise leader will expect change and be ready for it.

*The best moderation is shown when one is angry and the best forgiveness is shown when one is powerful.*

UMAR

## KEY POINTS

- *Humility at its simplest is knowing that you are not God.*

- *Being humble as a leader is essentially about not being arrogant.* According to the Arab proverb: *Arrogance diminishes wisdom.* A humble person, one who lacks all signs of pride both in spirit and in outward show, is walking on a path that leads to practical wisdom.

- *'Humility is just as much the opposite of self-abasement as it is of self-exaltation', wrote Dag Hammarskjöld, when he was Secretary-General of the United Nations.*

- *'Do not pursue a matter of which you are ignorant', counsels the Qur'an.* Wise leaders will consult their team before making a particular decision. They will listen especially to those who have technical knowledge or practical experience of the matter in hand.

- *'Let nothing prevent you from changing your previous decision', said Umar to his generals, 'if after consideration you feel that the previous decision was incorrect.'*

- The crown of a good disposition is humility, *says an Arab proverb, reflecting like a pearl both the light of the Qur'an and the iridescent spirit of Muhammad.*

*He who is deprived of his share of gentleness is deprived of his share of the good of this world and the next.*

MUHAMMAD

# 8

# From Past
# TO PRESENT

*Truth is the daughter of search.*

ARAB PROVERB

*Seek knowledge, even though it be in China.*

ARAB PROVERB

Saladin (Arabic: Salah-al-Din Yusuf ibn Ayyub) is the Muslim Arab leader best known to the West. Saladin earned an enduring reputation with friend and foe alike, not only for military skill but also for his integrity, courtesy and chivalry. As a leader, both in war and peace, Saladin exemplified the ideal of Muslim leadership that we have seen taking shape in this book, the model or pattern that Muhammad had himself taught in his own life and left as his legacy to all those willing to take upon their shoulders the responsibility of leadership.

Sultan of Egypt and Syria, Saladin in 1187 invaded the Crusader kingdom, won a great victory at the Horns of

Hattin over the Christian knights, and reconquered Jerusalem. For a period he successfully withstood the force of the Third Crusade, which was led by among others the king of England, Richard the Lionheart. Richard defeated the Saracen army four years later at Arsuf. Saladin withdrew to Damascus, where he died two years later.

Let me pick out one or two instances where we can see the light of the leadership of Muhammad distantly reflected in Saladin.

Take the Quranic principle of moderation, as in: 'Make not your hands tied (like a niggard's) to your neck, nor stretch it forth to its utmost reach, so that you become blameworthy and destitute' (Q17:29). Aristotle has also located virtue as the middle course between two extremes. The Romans called it the golden mean (Latin: *aurea mediocritas*, a phrase from Horace's *Odes*). Saladin, for example, was neither too brave in battle for his own good nor too anxious for his life. He struck just the right balance.

Before a battle Saladin – so a biographer who knew him well tells us – would traverse the whole army from the right wing to the left, creating a sense of unity and urging them to advance and stand firm at the right time. Once the armies engaged he would calmly ride between battle lines of his soldiers, under fire from bolts and arrows, accompanied only by a groom with a spare horse. Notice that he was in the zone of danger, but avoided foolishly throwing away his own life in hand-to-hand fighting. That is not the proper work of a general. By sharing their danger, being among them, he both steadied and calmed them. His very presence was inspiring. Dead generals cannot do that.

During a long truce Saladin conferred with Hubert Walter, Bishop of Salisbury, who happened to be on pilgrimage at the time. Saladin had observed King Richard in action and admired his courage. Richard was 20 years younger than the Saracen commander-in-chief, and he always threw himself into the thick of a battle. Through the bishop Saladin sent Richard some personal advice. 'Do not incur danger so unnecessarily', he urged him. 'Don't be so prodigal with your life!' Alas, Richard did not listen. Nor were the two generals destined to meet. Later, at a siege in France, Richard paid the price of not paying heed to a master in the art of generalship. He rushed needlessly into danger once too often and died from his wounds after being struck by an arrow. He was only 42. Saladin's advice to his young opponent was a kind thought, the sign of a magnanimous character.

Jerusalem was now once again in Muslim hands. During the truce with the Crusaders in 1191 and 1192, Saladin was preoccupied in strengthening the defences of the city that the Arabs called *al-Quds*, the holy place. He rode there from his camp before dawn, not returning some-times until midnight. He spent some of the night hours on his paperwork. Leaders need to be full of energy! He personally supervised the building work, 'even carrying stones on his own shoulders, and everybody, rich and poor, followed his example'. Like Muhammad before him, Saladin led from the front.

A Baghdad physician, Abd al-Latif, was with Saladin at this time and recalled him listening with pleasure and taking part in conversations at large meetings of learned scholars and scientists: 'I found him a great prince, whose appearance inspired at once respect and love, and who was approachable, deeply intellectual, gracious and noble in his thoughts. All who came near him took him as their model...'

One of his closest advisers, Baha al-Din, shared this view: 'Our Sultan', he wrote, 'was very noble of heart; kindness shone in his face; he was very modest and exquisitely courteous.'

Not long before his death Saladin wrote a letter of advice to his son, who was about to become a provincial governor for the first time. It illustrates his own philosophy of leadership:

*Abstain from the shedding of blood; trust not to that, for blood that is spilt never slumbers. Seek to win the hearts of your people, and watch over their prosperity. For it is to secure their happiness that you are appointed by God and by me. Try to gain the hearts of your emirs and ministers and nobles. I have become as great as I am because I have won men's hearts by gentleness and kindness.*

When Saladin died on 3 March 1193 in Damascus, where his tomb is to be found today, his physician wrote of him: 'All men grieved for him as they grieve for prophets. I have seen no other ruler for whose death the people mourned, for he was loved by good and bad, Muslims and unbelievers alike.'

Some 200 years after Saladin, Timur Leng and his army – Mongols and Turks – conquered a large area including Persia, Syria and northern India. Timur Leng, literally 'lame Timur', was known in the West as Tamerlane. Samarkand was his capital, but he died far from it while invading China. The Mogul dynasty in India was his legacy.

While besieging Damascus in 1400, Timur heard the news that the famous Islamic scholar Ibn Khaldun was in the city. Ibn Khaldun, a historian and philosopher of rare distinction, had accepted an invitation from the sultan of Egypt to accompany him on a military expedition to relieve the siege of Damascus. He was sent ahead with a small group of envoys to negotiate with the Mongol leader. As a consequence he found himself holed up in the city along with its hungry inhabitants. Eventually Timur sent word that he was willing to receive him, so Ibn Khaldun had himself lowered from the lofty city walls in a basket and found his way to Timur's tent. He then spent six weeks in the Mongol encampment, discussing a range of subjects with Timur that he listed in his autobiography. He added a vivid thumbnail sketch of his host:

*The King Timur is one of the greatest and mightiest of Kings. Some attribute to him knowledge, others attribute to him heresy… still others attribute to him the employment of magic and sorcery, but in all this there is nothing; it is simply that he is highly intelligent and perspicacious, addicted to debate and argumentation about what he knows and also about what he does not know.*

Notice the cool, objective eye of a born observer and thinker. Ibn Khaldun's great work, the *History of the World*, fills seven volumes. It opens with a statement that is still an exciting vision of what writing history is all about:

*History is a discipline widely cultivated among nations and races. It is eagerly sought after. The men in the street, the ordinary people, aspire to know it. Kings and leaders vie for it. Both the learned and the ignorant are able to understand it. For on the surface history is no more than information about political events, dynasties and occurrences of the remote past elegantly presented... The inner meaning of history, on the other hand, involves speculation and an attempt to get at the truth, subtle explanation of the causes and origins of existing things, and deep knowledge of the how and why of events. [History,] therefore, is firmly rooted in philosophy. It deserves to be accounted a branch of [philosophy].*

Humans are at the centre of Ibn Khaldun's world. And he follows the Greek geographers in relating humans to their physical environment. The influence of God in human affairs is limited to the extraordinary, for instance the prophetic interventions, of which the most important was His message to humankind through Muhammad.

People form themselves into society, which may be guided by prophecy, in order to achieve their full potential. In doing so they form *umran*, civilization. Civilizations, Ibn Khaldun tells us, take different forms according to their environment: *badawa*, desert or nomadic life, and *hadara*, sedentary or urban life.

About the Bedouin inhabitants of the desert Ibn Khaldun is ambivalent. On the one hand they are 'the most savage people on earth, who therefore plunder and cause damage – preferring to do so without having to fight or to expose themselves'. On the other hand, he writes, 'clearly the Bedouin are closer to being good than sedentary people'.

Western pilgrims to the Holy Land could see only the savage and rapacious side of the Bedouin. The English pilgrim and traveller Sir John De Mandeville, writing in 1322, 10 years before the birth of Ibn Khaldun, had not a good word to say about them: 'In that desert dwelt many of the Arabians who are called Bedouins... who are a people full of all evil conditions. They are strong and warlike men, and they are right felonious and foul, and of a cursed nature.' It was not until the 18th and 19th centuries, when English travellers found their way into the Arabian desert and lived among the Bedouin, that they saw – like Ibn Khaldun – the other side of the coin.

The Bedouin, continued Ibn Khaldun, are 'more inclined towards goodness and good qualities' than their settled neighbours. The qualities of their tribal leaders, 'which have made them deserving of being leaders of the people', are reflections of the good qualities of the Bedouin tribesmen. They include 'generosity, the forgiveness of error, tolerance towards the weak, hospitality towards guests, the support of dependents, maintenance of the needy, patience in adverse circumstances, faithful fulfilment of obligations, liberality with money for the preservation of honour, humility towards the poor, avoidance of fraud, deceit or cunning, and shirking of obligations'.

Not that the Bedouins were ever easy to lead. They were not natural team players, being strongly individual. 'For every Bedouin is eager to be the leader,' writes Ibn Khaldun. 'There is scarcely one among them who would cede his power to another, even to his father, his brother, or to the eldest member of his family.' Some might say that the characteristic of each Arab wanting to be the leader – with a consequent lack of effective teamwork – has endured to this day. An Arab may leave the desert, but the desert never leaves an Arab.

Yet Ibn Khaldun observed how Islam had the power to transform the Bedouin's characteristics of being rude, proud, and ambitious to be the leader. Where there is religion among them, 'the qualities of haughtiness and jealousy leave them'. Even so, the nomadic tribesmen needed a particular style of leadership. 'Their leader needs them [the Bedouins] mostly for the group spirit that is necessary for purposes of defence. He is, therefore, forced to rule them kindly and to avoid antagonizing them. Otherwise he would have trouble with the group spirit, resulting in his undoing and theirs.'

Ibn Khaldun takes it as a fundamental principle that human beings are made to cooperate. Central to success in cooperation is what he calls *asabiya*, the 'group feeling' or 'group spirit'. Having more *asabiya* makes one group superior to another. Leaders who can command it to best effect will be stronger than their rivals and will even be able to form new dynasties and new states.

But, as history shows, Ibn Khaldun argued, success ultimately breeds luxury and degeneration in the sedentary existence, *asabiyah* weakens, and the urban world becomes exposed to those peoples, usually in the nomadic world, who can command greater *asabiya*. Doubtless this was among the subjects Ibn Khaldun discussed with Timur, the leader of hordes of nomads and the destroyer of cities. Thus all dynastic history moved in circles. Ibn Khaldun's *Muqaddima* was ultimately a reflection on power.

There is no exact equivalent in English to the Arabic word *asabiya*. It encompasses group cohesiveness, *esprit de corps*, ethos, morale, identity, confidence, discipline and collective aspiration: everything, in fact, that makes a group into a whole that is more than the sum of its parts, everything that gives it direction and impels it to seek power.

Ibn Khaldun does, as we have seen, make a connection with leadership, but his emphasis is very much on the *group* and its rising (or falling) power or spirit rather than upon the leadership of the leader. Leaders cannot remain effective when their people have lost their former *asabiya*. You can understand why some Western writers have hailed Ibn Khaldun as the father of sociology.

It is certainly possible to overemphasize the part of any particular leader – or leaders – in the success of a given group. Leadership is only one factor, though a self-evidently important one.

*Ten soldiers wisely led,*
*Will beat a hundred without a head.*

EURIPIDES

That is true, but one could argue – in the tradition of Ibn Khaldun – that it is the *asabiya* of the 10 soldiers, not to mention their training and skill, that counts as much as who led them from the front. At the battle of Badr, when 300 Muslims fought 1,000 soldiers from Mecca and won, they did so not simply because they had good leadership, but because their faith in God outranked that of their opponents.

In order to remain humble, leaders should remember the Scottish proverb: *The clan is always greater than the chief.* It reinforces the notion that as a leader you are there to serve your group or organization, not to impose your greatness upon them but to identify, nurture, draw out and channel *their* greatness.

Although it may be fanciful, we could see Ibn Khaldun as the forerunner of social psychology, the psychology of groups as opposed to individuals. In this field today working groups are seen as wholes that are more than the sum of their parts. They have a life, as it were, of their own. Like individuals, groups – if they have been together – develop a *group personality* that is unique. But they also share elements in common. It is the study of the universal elements in groups that led me to discover the generic role of *leader*, and I shall leave you with a brief sketch of that approach.

The discovery I was referring to is a simple one: that in all working groups there are three interactive *areas of need* that lead us finally to the elusive goal – the universal role of *leader*. They are:

- the need to accomplish the common task;

- the need to be maintained or held together as a working and cohesive group or team;

- the needs that individuals bring with them into the working group by virtue of being individual persons.

As the Chinese proverb says: *A picture is worth a thousand words* (see Figure 8.1).

You may like to explore some of the possible interactions. If you place a coin over the 'Task' circle in Figure 8.1, it will immediately cover segments of the other two circles as well. In other words, lack of task or failure to achieve it will affect both team maintenance – increasing disruptive tendencies – and the area of individual needs, lowering member satisfaction within the group. Move the coin on to the 'Team' circle and again the impact of a near-complete lack of relationships in the group on both task and individual needs may be seen at a glance.

Conversely, when a group achieves its task the degree of group cohesiveness and enjoyment of membership should go up. Morale, both corporate and individual, will

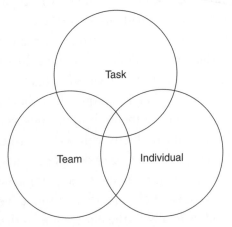

Figure 8.1 *The interaction of areas of need*

be higher. And if the members of a group happen to get on extremely well together and find that they can work closely as a team, this will increase their work performance and also meet some important needs that individuals bring with them into common life.

These three interlocking circles therefore illustrate the general point that each area of need exerts an influence upon the other two; they do not form watertight compartments.

Clearly, in order that the group should fulfil its task and be held together as a working team, certain *functions* will have to be performed. By 'function' in this context I mean any behaviour, words or actions that meet one or more spheres of 'need', or *areas of leadership responsibility* as they may also be called. Defining the aim, planning, controlling, evaluating, supporting and encouraging the group are examples of what is meant by the word *function* in this context. A quality is what you are; a function is what you *do*. And each function can be performed with more or less skill.

*Vision without a task is merely a dream,*
*A task without vision is simply drudgery,*
*Vision with action can change the world.*

ANONYMOUS

The generic role of leader centres upon the responsibility for these necessary functions. That doesn't mean to say that leaders have to do everything themselves – there are anyway too many functions needed in a group for any one person to provide them all. The good leader treats team members as leaders in their own right. He or she is a 'leader of leaders'.

Take decision making, for example. The general principle is that the more you share decisions with your team the better, for the people involved will feel more committed to carrying them out. But there are natural factors – shortage of time, extent of knowledge and experience of the group or individual – that may limit how far you can go.

Why is it that a group perceives and accepts one person as a leader rather than someone else? We now have a working answer to that key question:

*A leader is the sort of person with the appropriate qualities and knowledge – which is more than technical or professional – who is able to provide the necessary functions to enable a team to achieve its task and to hold it together as a working unity. And this is done not by the leader alone but by eliciting the contributions and willing cooperation of all involved.*

There is a useful distinction to be made between an *organization* and a *community*, though both are the products of humans imposing order on chaos. A community derives from the family, kindred group or tribe and has order through acceptance of common law and a form of government. Our nation states stand in this line of descent. Organizations, by contrast, are hunting parties at large. They are formed and developed with a particular form of work or – in the most general sense – task in mind.

Lastly, it is worth bearing in mind that leadership takes place on different levels:

- *Team:* The leader of a team of some 10 to 20 people with clearly specified tasks to achieve.

- *Operational:* The leader of one of the main parts of the organization, with more than one team leader under one's control. It is already a case of being a leader of leaders.

- *Strategic:* The leader of a whole organization, with a number of operational leaders under one's personal direction.

A simple recipe for organizational success is to have effective leaders occupying these roles and working together in harmony as a team. That is simple enough to say: I am not implying that it is easy either to achieve or to maintain that state of affairs under the pressures of life today.

Above I have set out for you the generic role of leader. It is simply what human beings – at all times and in all places – expect of their leaders. Although according to the Qur'an it was Allah who created unity (Q3:103, 8:63) among believers, Muhammad worked harder towards that end than any other leader. He enabled the Muslim community that had been called into being to set and achieve tasks, to live and work together in harmony. Under his leadership the *Muhajirun* (Emigrants) and the *Ansar* (Helpers) eventually came together as one – the *Ashab* (Companions or Supporters) of the Prophet. And he gave all individual members new hope that their deepest needs would be met, in the next world if not in this one.

We think of great leaders like Muhammad inspiring their people, but inspiration is often mutual. Rather than thinking of leaders creating groups or organizations in their own image, we should think now of organizations, communities and nations seeking leaders who will meet their high expectations, who will share their values and vision.

*As you are like, so will your rulers be.*

ARAB PROVERB

# KEY POINTS

- *You can be appointed a ruler, governor, commander or manager, but you are not a* leader *until your appointment is ratified in the hearts and minds of those under you.*

- *Reciprocity is a* fundamental *law in all personal or social relations.* What you give as a leader will be what you tend to receive. As an Arab proverb says, *He who would be loved must begin by loving.*

- *A good leader is someone whom people will follow through thick and thin, in good times and bad, because they have confidence in the leader as a person, the leader's ability and his or her knowledge of the job and because they know they matter to the leader.*

- *Apart from exemplifying the qualities and values of their group, leaders should have the generic qualities of leadership:* enthusiasm, integrity, firmness and fairness, resilience, warmth or humanity, and humility.

- *The nature of the field or context does affect leadership:* different fields of work call for different leaders. A leader needs to have the necessary knowledge or experience, for *authority flows to the one who knows.*

- *The three intersecting circles point you to the generic role of leader.* You can always improve your skills in performing the necessary functions. Leadership is about *doing* – it is action centred. Fulfil the role of leader and let your qualities look after themselves.

*What one does, one becomes.*

SPANISH PROVERB

# CONCLUSION

Every reader is different. I have written this book for you personally, and I hope that you have enjoyed it. Now I invite you to take away from it whatever pearls of wisdom and spurs to action you need. Only you can know what they are. Your way lies before you.

As I have indicated more than once, thanks to the long search for truth there is now a global body of knowledge about leadership and leadership development. We do know what is the generic term of leader. We can now clothe it with flesh and blood drawn from three great traditions: Western thought beginning with Socrates; Eastern thought as exemplified by Confucius; and the Tribal tradition, its wisdom coming down to us mainly in the form of proverbs.

This book in part has been about the Tribal tradition of leadership, for there have been few finer exemplars of it than the Bedouin tribes of Arabia. Muhammad was a product of Bedouin society but he also, as we have seen, transcended it.

The Muslim tradition of leadership, if I have understood it, transcends even the three great human traditions of understanding leadership that I have just mentioned. At its pinnacle is the lofty ideal that human leaders – men and women, boys and girls – should model themselves on God. Through meditation on the Qur'an, Muslims should seek to reflect in their way of life – especially in their leadership – these qualities in the world, as the moon reflects the sun.

If your feet stand in the Muslim tradition, then that may be the path for you – the way in which you can grow to be a 'good leader and a leader for good'. But within Islamic thought there is a bridge between theology and philosophy – a bridge that made possible the flowering of Islamic science, mathematics and historical scholarship in the Middle Ages. That bridge, of course, is the concept of Truth. For truth is truth, whether it is found by contemplating the names of God or through the study of human nature and social life, which is the road that I have travelled. Therefore Islam today is both an inheritor of the world's body of knowledge about leadership and – as I trust that I have shown in this book – a great contributor to it.

How often did Muhammad have to remind people that he was just a man? In other words, he was as much an inhabitant of a local time and place – with all that entails – as you and I are in our here and now. We have to live in our day as Muhammad lived in his day.

What I do believe, however, is that, different as we all are in this world, we can now all learn to lead – just as Muhammad developed as a leader. Indeed learning and leadership go hand in hand. You are not born a leader; you become one. It is never too late to learn. Practical wisdom tells us, however, that the sooner you start on that inner journey of learning to lead, the better for you and for those whom you are called to save.

*Learning in old age is written on sand,*
*but learning in youth is engraved on stone.*

ARAB PROVERB

Before we part company there is one other conclusion that I want to share with you, although it is not strictly relevant to this book. It will not come as a surprise to you if you happen to be a Muslim. It is this: Islam is a religion of love. As Ibn al-Arabi (died 1240), known also as al-Shaykh al-Akbar, 'the greatest sheikh', said: 'Love is the faith I hold: wherever turn its camels, still the one true faith is mine.' That Love should own camels is a very Bedouin thought! Ibn al-Arabi is usually classified as a Sufi – so named for their woollen robes – who had a strong mystical tradition. Who else but a mystic could write: 'Love is the shadow of God'?

But even within the mainstream of Islamic thought we find a sense of Islam being a religion of love. Omar Khayyam, who lived a hundred years before Ibn al-Arabi, is well known in the world as the author of the *Ruba'iyyat*. Early Arabic and Persian sources consistently describe him as a philosopher, astronomer and mathematician, and he is known to have devised a new and more accurate calendar. In other words, he exemplified the Islamic intellectual virtues.

Many of the hundreds of *ruba'iyyat* (Arabic: quatrains) – stanzas with four lines – attributed to Omar Khayyam are spurious, but I like to think that the one I am going to leave you with is genuine, that it is an *al-Jiwan*, a great and lustrous pearl of the Arabian seas:

*The heart that love and charity do leaven*
*Whether to mosque or church its praise is given*
*His name that is written in the Book of Love,*
*What fears he Hell, what care has he for Heaven?*

*Ma' as-salaam*, Go in peace.

# APPENDIX: A BRIEF LIFE OF MUHAMMAD

Muhammad was born *c*570 CE, the son of Abdullah, a poor merchant but in an honoured family of the powerful tribe of the Quraysh, hereditary guardians of the shrine in Mecca in Arabia. He was orphaned by the age of 6, and brought up first by his grandfather and then by his uncle, Abu Talib. He worked as a shepherd and then as a caravan leader. At the age of 24 he worked in this capacity for a wealthy widow, Khadija (died *c*618), whom he eventually married. They had six children, but no sons survived. Their daughters included Umm Kulthum and Fatima, whose husbands Uthman and Ali became respectively the third and fourth caliphs.

While continuing as Khadija's agent or caravan leader Muhammad became increasingly drawn to religious contemplation. It was in 610, the traditional year, that Muhammad spent a time of prayer and fasting in the mountains outside Mecca. There he experienced the vastness of the rocky waste, the purity of the keen air, the beauty at dawn and sunset, the wonderful starlit nights and the profound silence and stillness.

One night, while resting in a cave on Mount Hira wrapped in his cloak, he encountered Gabriel and experienced the first divine revelation (Q96: 1–5) as the Qur'an says.

Muhammad may have received messages in a vision, as did the prophet Isaiah (Isaiah 6), or heard God speak through what the Hebrews called the *bath-gol*, the heavenly voice (Hebrew: daughter of the voice). Or he may have heard Him through an angel intermediary such as the archangel Gabriel (Hebrew: *gavri 'el*, strong man of God), one of the seven archangels in Hebrew tradition. Or he may have received the inspired words as if from a still, small voice speaking from the depths of his unconscious mind – a phenomenon well attested in poetic and musical composition. Which of these possibilities is true only God knows. They are not mutually exclusive. But I should add, however, that Muhammad always denied that he was a poet.

These oracles, later preserved in writing in the Qur'an (Arabic: recitation, proclamation), commanded that the numerous idols in and around the shrine known as *al-Ka'ba* (Arabic: cube) should be destroyed and that the rich should show more generosity to the poor. This simple message attracted some support but provoked a great deal of hostility from those who felt that their cherished beliefs, their traditional way of life and possibly their commercial interests were being threatened.

When his wife Khadija died, Muhammad was reduced to poverty. His uncle's death also made him insecure, for he had lost the all-important protection of his clan. Some of his supporters had already taken refuge in Abyssinia. Muhammad had made a handful of converts among Bedouin pilgrims to Mecca, notably from the two half-nomadic tribes based in the oasis settlement of Yathrib, which lay some 350 kilometres to the north. By 622, when Muhammad's personal safety in Mecca was in jeopardy, he was ready to accept their offer of hospitality and protection. He migrated there, and this migration, the

Hegira (Arabic: *hijra*, dissociation or migration), was taken as the beginning of the Muslim era. Yathrib is better known as Medina (Arabic: to city).

The most important decision of the leaders of the young Muslim community – an amalgam of Qurayshite Muhajirun (Arabic: emigrants) and Ansar (Arabic: helpers or allies) drawn from the two Arab tribes in Medina – was to make war against the perceived actual or potential enemies of Islam, starting with the polytheistic Meccans.

In March 624 a small force of Muslims defeated a small Meccan army at Badr. A year later, however, Muhammad almost lost his life in a battle against the same foe at Uhud. In 627 the Muslims survived a siege of Medina by the Meccans. By 629, however, Muhammad was able to take control of Mecca; it recognized him as both its master and the Messenger of God. Over the next two years he extended his domain over almost all of Arabia. In March 632 he undertook his farewell pilgrimage to Mecca, and there on Mount Arafat fixed for all time the ceremonies of the pilgrimage.

Muhammad fell ill soon after his return and died on 8 June in the home of the favourite of his nine wives, Aisha, the daughter of one of his first followers, Abu Bakr. His tomb in the mosque at Medina is venerated throughout Islam. Abu Bakr became the first caliph or successor, followed by three other early companions: Umar, Uthman and Muhammad's son-in-law Ali.

You should bear in mind that the earliest written source for the origins of Islam is the Qur'an, which reached its definitive form during the caliphate of Uthman (644–56).

There are references to historical events – such as the battles of Badr, Uhud and Hunayn – but they are sparse and there is relatively little about Muhammad.

The first written biographies appeared about a hundred years later. The most notable of them is by Muhammad ibn Ishaq (died 767). Another influential early historian was Muhammad al-Waqidi. His *Kitab al-Maghazi* (Book of the Conquests) records the Prophet's alleged presence and part in some 28 military raids and battles out of over 70 that occurred during the last decade of his life.

Arabs were noted for their exceptional memories, but stories handed down orally over such a long period are bound to get distorted or elaborated, with details supplied by talented and imaginative storytellers as they filled the gaps. Therefore some caution is wise, and historians have to use their professional knowledge, experience and intuition.

When it comes to the *hadith* (Arabic: tradition, especially the body of tradition relating to the sayings and doings of Muhammad), a rigorous attempt to grade them like pearls in terms of quality (reliability, authenticity, veracity) was made as early as Umar (the Umayyad caliph who ruled between 717 and 720), for they formed the basis with the Qur'an for Islamic law. In establishing their pedigrees the Arabs applied their skills as genealogists.

Most of the 650,000 alleged sayings of the Prophet fall outside the canon. An acceptable *hadith* is composed of two parts: the main text and a chain of authorities – of its genealogy – reporting it. The first in the chain has to be one of the Companions (Arabic: *sahaba*, related to *sahib*, companion) of Muhammad, his close associates who converted to Islam at various times. The majority of scholars count as Companions all those Muslims alive in his generation who had contact with him, however fleeting. The two most famous collections of *hadiths* are by Bukhari (810–70) and Muslim al-Hajjaj (817–75). If a saying appears in both of them it has a very good pedigree.

*Ma' as-salama*, Go in peace.

# ABOUT THE AUTHOR

John Adair is one of the world's leading authorities on leadership and leadership development. Over a million managers worldwide have taken part in the Action-Centred Leadership programmes he pioneered.

John had a colourful early career. He served as a platoon commander in the Scots Guards in Egypt, and then became the only national serviceman to serve in the Arab Legion, where he became adjutant of a Bedouin regiment. After national service he qualified as a deckhand in Hull and worked on an arctic trawler in Iceland waters. He then worked as a hospital orderly in the operating theatre of a hospital.

After being senior lecturer in military history and adviser in leadership training at the Royal Military Academy Sandhurst, and Associate Director of The Industrial Society, in 1979 John became the world's first

Professor of Leadership Studies at the University of Surrey.

Between 1981 and 1986 John worked with Sir John Harvey-Jones at ICI introducing a leadership development strategy that helped to change the loss-making, bureaucratic giant into the first British company to make a billion pounds profit.

John has written over 40 books, translated into many languages. His recent books, published by Kogan Page, include *Not Bosses But Leaders*, *The Inspirational Leader*, *How to Grow Leaders* and *Leadership and Motivation*. Apart from being an author he is also a teacher and consultant.

From St Paul's School he won a scholarship to Cambridge University. John holds the higher degrees of Master of Letters from Oxford University and Doctor of Philosophy from King's College London, and he is also a Fellow of the Royal Historical Society. Recently the People's Republic of China awarded him the title of Honorary Professor in recognition of his 'outstanding research and contribution in the field of Leadership'.

In 2009, John was appointed Chair of Leadership Studies United Nations System Staff College in Turin.

# INDEX

# Also available from **Kogan Page**

Find out more; visit **www.koganpage.com** and
sign up for offers and regular e-newsletters.

# Also available from **Kogan Page**

# Also available from **Kogan Page**

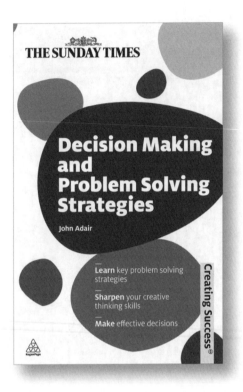

Find out more; visit **www.koganpage.com** and
sign up for offers and regular e-newsletters.

# Also available from **Kogan Page**

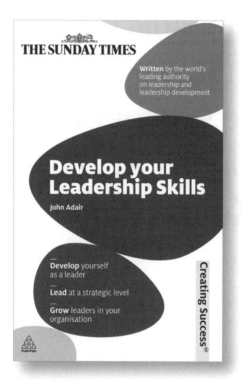

Find out more; visit **www.koganpage.com** and
sign up for offers and regular e-newsletters.

With over 42 years of publishing, more than 80 million people have succeeded in business with thanks to **Kogan Page**

# www.koganpage.com

**KoganPage**